PARAGON ISSUES IN PHILOSOPHY

PARAGON ISSUES IN PHILOSOPHY

FORTHCOMING TITLES

THE PARAGON ISSUES IN PHILOSOPHY SERIES

At colleges and universities, interest in the traditional areas of philosophy remains strong. Many new currents flow within them, too, but some of these—the rise of cognitive science, for example, or feminist philosophy—went largely unnoticed in undergraduate philosophy courses until the end of the 1980s. The Paragon Issues in Philosophy Series responds to both perennial and newly influential concerns by bringing together a team of able philosophers to address the fundamental issues in philosophy today and to outline the state of contemporary discussion about them.

More than twenty volumes are scheduled; they are organized into three major categories. The first covers the standard topics—metaphysics, theory of knowledge, ethics, and political philosophy—stressing innovative developments in those disciplines. The second focuses on more specialized but still vital concerns in the philosophies of science, religion, history, sport, and other areas. The third category explores new work that relates philosophy and fields such as feminist criticism, medicine, economics, technology, and literature.

The level of writing is aimed at undergraduate students who have little previous experience studying philosophy. The books provide brief but accurate introductions that appraise the state of the art in their fields and show how the history of thought about their topics developed. Each volume is complete in itself but also complements others in the series.

Traumatic change characterizes these last years of the twentieth century: all of it involves philosophical issues. The editorial staff at Paragon House has worked with us to develop this series. We hope it will encourage the understanding needed in our times, which are as complicated and problematic as they are promising.

John K. Roth   Frederick Sontag
Claremont McKenna College   Pomona College

PHILOSOPHY

OF

SPORT

ALSO BY DREW HYLAND

The Origins of Philosophy, 1973

The Virtue of Philosophy, 1981

The Question of Play, 1984

DREW A. HYLAND

TRINITY COLLEGE
HARTFORD, CONNECTICUT

PHILOSOPHY
OF
SPORT

PARAGON
ISSUES IN
PHILOSOPHY

PARAGON HOUSE · NEW YORK

FIRST EDITION, 1990

PUBLISHED IN THE UNITED STATES BY

PARAGON HOUSE
90 FIFTH AVENUE
NEW YORK, NY 10011

COPYRIGHT © 1990 BY PARAGON HOUSE

SERIES DESIGN BY KATHY KIKKERT.

LIBRARY OF CONGRESS CATALOGING-IN-PUBLICATION DATA

HYLAND, DREW A.
    PHILOSOPHY OF SPORT / DREW A. HYLAND. — 1ST ED.
    P.   CM. — (PARAGON ISSUES IN PHILOSOPHY)
    INCLUDES BIBLIOGRAPHICAL REFERENCES.
    ISBN 1-55778-189-3
    1. SPORTS—PHILOSOPHY. I. TITLE. II. SERIES.
  GV706.H95   1990
  796'.01—DC20   90-31113
                                                      CIP

THE PAPER USED IN THIS PUBLICATION MEETS THE MINIMUM
REQUIREMENTS OF AMERICAN NATIONAL STANDARD FOR
INFORMATION SCIENCES—PERMANENCE OF PAPER FOR PRINTED
LIBRARY MATERIAL, ANSI Z39.48-1984.

MANUFACTURED IN THE UNITED STATES OF AMERICA
10 9 8 7 6 5 4 3 2 1

FOR THOSE WHO KNOW
THAT THEY HAVE SOULS AND BODIES,
AND WHO LOVE BOTH.

CONTENTS

Chariots of Fire use ?

assign O'Brian article also

PREFACE

There is a long tradition that calls on the academy, as one of its central tasks, to reflect on and analyze social phenomena that play an important role in a given culture. Thus, there are many and varied considerations of the role of politics, religion, music, and the arts by the various disciplines in the academy, certainly including philosophy. Arguably, however, that social phenomenon in American life which has the biggest impact on our culture, yet which receives the least serious attention from our intellectual standard-bearers, is sport and athletics. There seems to be a long-standing prejudice that however popular a phenomenon sport may be, however widely its influence may permeate our culture, it is simply not "serious" enough to be a legitimate subject of intellectual inquiry. That has certainly been one of the long-standing prejudices of professional philosophy.

read

I hope that this book takes at least a small step toward attacking and overcoming that academic prejudice, which, obviously, I regard as entirely unjustified. There is much that is important, serious, and thought-provoking about sport, and this book is intended to focus on at least some of those important issues which deserve thoughtful consideration.

The book is directed toward two audiences, one more general than the other. The larger audience is the hopefully large and growing number of thoughtful people for whom, perhaps, sport has played a significant role in their own lives, or who are at least interested in sport and the role it plays in our society. The book will also be especially helpful to those students and faculty members who are making the study of sport and its significance for human being an explicit part of their intellectual enterprise. There are, happily, a growing number of courses on the philosophy of sport in colleges and universities throughout the country, and this book is intended to be a contribution to the philosophic literature useful to those scholars and students.

There are a number of people who have been especially helpful to me in formulating the ideas and arguments of this book. First and foremost are the large number of students in my philosophy of sport course over the years, whose challenging questions and helpful suggestions have been decisive in my coming to hold the positions that I take herein. The editors at Paragon House and the two series editors, John Roth and Fred Sontag, have offered many helpful suggestions and criticisms, as have the two readers of the manuscript, Joy DeSensi and John Doody. I have adopted many of their recommendations, for which I am most grateful. My colleague and friend, Miller Brown, read part of the manuscript and offered important suggestions as well. Finally, my wife, Anne, and my sons, Christopher and Craig—who still pick me on their teams even though I cost them many a game—have listened to the ideas presented in this book over the years, and their responses and criticisms inform page after page. To them and for them I am most thankful of all.

INTRODUCTION

In recent years, a growing number of philosophers and students of philosophy have been turning their attention to a set of issues joined loosely under the rubric "the philosophy of sport." Books and articles are being published in the area, courses are being taught under this title, and there is even a flourishing interdisciplinary organization, The Philosophical Society for the Study of Sport, which meets regularly to address issues within this field. All this seems perfectly plausible; sport almost always has played a significant role in our culture and in other cultures, and one of the things that philosophers often do is turn their attention to those activities and phenomena which are central to a given culture. Philosophy of sport would not in this respect seem to be significantly different from, say, the philosophy of science, or the philosophy of religion, or the philosophy of art, each of which have long been staples of the offerings of most philosophy departments.

In a book on the philosophy of art, or science, or religion, one might expect the author to begin with a review of the major positions taken on the subject by the great philosophers of the past. In these subjects one would have little difficulty going back to Plato or even to the Pre-Socratic philosophers to survey their responses to these issues. Here we confront the first anomaly in the philosophy of sport. The "history" of work in the philosophy of sport is sparse indeed. Prior to this century, there are almost no works by important philosophers focusing on philosophic issues of sport or play. At most, as we shall consider presently, we find occasional remarks, almost in passing, by philosophers such as Plato, Aristotle, or Nietzsche, usually treating sport or play as an example of a broader point—or as a metaphor for a larger issue being addressed.

This might be understandable if ours were one of the first cultures in which sport played a significant role. Were that true, it would hardly be surprising that the study of sport had not been taken up explicitly by thinkers of the past. But as the historian, Johan Huizinga, has pointed out in persuasive detail, sport or play has almost always played a central role, not only in our own culture, but in virtually every culture of which we are aware. Indeed, the central thesis of Huizinga's great book on the subject, *Homo Ludens*, is that ". . . civilization arises and unfolds in and as play."[1] It can thus hardly be the case that sport never has played a cultural role that called for the philosopher's attention. It is as if a massive prejudice has pervaded the history of philosophy, that although such issues as religion, art, or science clearly deserve the philosopher's attention, "mere" sport is not serious enough to be worthy of thematic treatment. That prejudice would seem to have been at least partially overcome in this century, especially in recent years.

But as indicated earlier, older philosophers, some of the greatest, have at least touched on philosophical aspects of sport and play, even if not in a sustained way. A number of Plato's dialogues (the *Lysis* and *Charmides*, for example) take place in a gymnasium, the place not only of physical training but also of intellectual and moral education in ancient Athens. If we can believe Diogenes Laertius, Socrates "paid great attention to the training of the body, and was always in excellent condition himself," while Plato even participated in the Isthmian games as a wrestler.[2] In the *Republic*, Socrates emphasizes the indispensability of gymnastic training in a good education,[3] and in the *Laws*, the Athenian Stranger praises play as the very highest of human activities.[4] Thus even though he does not address a whole dialogue explicitly to the theme, Plato does demonstrate an awareness of the importance of sport to human life. Similarly, Aristotle occasionally employs athletes as examples for points he wishes to make.

After the Greeks, precious little is said by philosophers about sport and play until the 19th century, when Nietzsche begins to use play as an important metaphor for the purposeless, irrational "happening" of things as "will to power," and for the human life he wishes to recommend. However, the sense of play that Nietzsche has in mind refers less to the rule-governed, goal-oriented play of the athlete than to the purposeless, spontaneous play of the child. Commenting on the famous fragment 52 of Heraclitus ("Time [or lifetime: *aion*] is a child playing, playing at draughts. Kingship belongs to a child"), Nietzsche says,

In this world only play, play as artists and children engage in it, exhibits coming to be and passing away, structuring and destroying, without any moral additive, in forever equal innocence. And as children and artists play, so plays the everliving fire.[5]

After Nietzsche, a number of European philosophers, including Martin Heidegger, Hans-Georg Gadamer, Michel Foucault, and Jacques Derrida, employ the metaphor of child's play in similar ways.[6]

In the 20th century, in addition to the use of the metaphor of child's play by thinkers such as Heidegger, Foucault, and Derrida, we find other philosophers using sport and games as metaphors for important themes in their thought. The French philosopher Jean-Paul Sartre uses a description of the experience of skiing to make clear his important distinction between "being," "doing," and "having,"[7] and, philosophizing in the analytic tradition, Ludwig Wittgenstein employs the metaphor of "language games" as a decisive model for his understanding of language.[8]

It is also in the 20th century that thinkers begin to turn

attention directly to sport and play as themes for investigation. I have mentioned Huizinga's *Homo Ludens*, perhaps the single book that legitimated the study of sport as a serious intellectual enterprise. In addition to it, other works in disciplines at least tangential to philosophy, such as Eugen Herrigel's seminal *Zen in the Art of Archery*,[9] works in the sociology and psychology of sport, and some works, largely emanating from scholars in physical education departments on the philosophy of sport, increasingly gave legitimacy to the study of sport as a serious subject. Finally, in 1969, an eminent American philosopher, Paul Weiss, published a full-length book on sport entitled *Sport: A Philosophic Inquiry*.[10] This book has been widely praised and criticized, but it indisputably was the first recent book devoted explicitly to sport written by a well-known philosopher. It thereby established the philosophy of sport in the pantheon of philosophic subjects. Shortly thereafter, in 1972, the Philosophic Society for the Study of Sport was established, with Weiss as its founding president.

Clearly, then, the philosophy of sport as a formal philosophic discipline is one of the most recent "movements" in philosophy. What are some of the major issues treated under its aegis? I shall respond to this question by outlining the structure of this book, whose purpose is to set out in greater detail what some of the major issues and controversies in the philosophy of sport are.

Chapter 1 treats a congeries of issues having to do with the role that sport plays in society, with special emphasis on American society. It has often been observed that an indication of the significance of sport in American society can be gleaned by noting that the two largest sections devoted to a single subject in most daily newspapers are the business section and the sports section; it is a good guess that many people turn first to the sports! Sport clearly plays a significant cultural role in our society, but what are the philosophic issues contained therein?

One of the most important has to do with whether and to

what extent sports "teach values." One occasionally reads of a symposium or magazine article on the topic, "Do sports teach values?"—but that question is probably ill-formed. It seems that virtually everyone agrees that sports do teach values; the question is, are those values worth teaching or not? We are all familiar with the litany of virtues that the partisans of sport claim will be instilled in our youth through athletic participation: teamwork, discipline, the spirit of fair play, a strong, healthy body—the list could go on.

On the other hand, the harshest critics of sports seem persuaded that sports teach values too—all the wrong ones. Sports, we are told, help instill in our young people such "virtues" as a mindless obedience to authority, a win-at-all-costs attitude, a spirit of competitiveness which turns people on the other team into enemies who should be hurt, intimidated, and cheated, plus a willingness to ruin one's health if it will help one win. There is at least some evidence for both claims. We shall want to consider in some depth what the connection is between athletic participation and the inculcation of values, positive or negative.

Whatever the precise connection, it seems clear that society's values—again both the positive and negative ones—are at least reflected in the sporting community. The histories of racism and sexism in sport, to take important examples, are no less deplorable than in our society as a whole. Because of its more circumscribed nature, sport can offer us a focused look at these problems, how they have been perpetuated, and how they might be overcome. In addition, we shall discover that, because of the inherently physical nature of most sports, certain issues in the problem of sexism can be especially clarified.

On the other hand, it seems increasingly the case that the sports community is furnishing us with our cultural heroes. Outstanding athletes such as Jackie Kersee-Joyner, Michael Jordan, or, to use more problematic examples, Lawrence Taylor or Wade Boggs, are increasingly the idols of choice—and therefore of imitation—for our young people. Should we deplore this, lamenting, for example, that there seem no longer to be Washingtons and Lincolns for our youth to idolize? Or should we be consoled that at least we are no longer idolizing those particularly adept at killing other people—"war heroes"—and consider that a mark of a higher culture? In any case, just what is there about athletics that its outstanding participants are accorded hero status, and what are we to make of this?

Chapter 2, "Ethical Issues in Sport," focuses on a number of ethical issues. None of them are peculiar to sport, but the sporting situation presents us with particularly focused examples. Perhaps the most notorious of these at present is the increased—some would say epidemic—use of drugs in sport (particularly the use of performance-enhancing drugs such as anabolic steroids). Should we ban such drug use? Or following a more libertarian inclination, should we allow their use as long as there is "informed consent?" That majority who recommend banning usually appeal either to arguments based on the presumed health danger to the athletes, or to considerations of fairness which are supposedly violated when some athletes compete with the strength-enhancing benefits of steroids.

On the issue of health, we shall discover that the extent of risk from controlled steroid use is more controversial than many suppose. In any case, our society is remarkably inconsistent about our appeal to paternalistic arguments aimed at protecting the health of our citizens. Witness the flourishing cigarette industry, notwithstanding the clear knowledge of the health dangers smoking involves. As to the question of fairness, we shall discover that the determination of what constitutes "fairness" involves a number of complex and subtle philosophic issues.

A second area of ethical concern centers on the "winning isn't everything, it's the only thing" attitude that seems increasingly prevalent, especially in those highly organized and often financially rewarding sporting frameworks such as professional and intercollegiate athletics. On the one hand, we can all call forth slogans from the athletic realm designed to emphasize the desirability and the importance of winning: "Show me a good loser and I'll show you a loser," "Nice guys finish last," and the notorious "winning is the only thing" slogan quoted above, apparently mis-attributed to the late football coach, Vince Lombardi. Yet the consequences of actually living out these maxims in practice seems to have generated a situation nearly everyone finds deplorable. Cheating is rampant, not only in the game, when one can get away with it, but even and especially in preparation for winning the games. The ethical state of intercollegiate athletics is now in crisis, with recruiting violations of all sorts constantly in the headlines. If, as surely seems the case, these problems are directly related to an exaggerated emphasis on winning, how is that emphasis to be controlled? How does one establish a "healthy" emphasis on winning? Indeed, is there such a thing? Can we eliminate these problems without eliminating athletic competition altogether? And should we consider that Draconian solution?

Considerations such as these will lead us to the problem of competition itself. Karl Marx argued long ago that competition in the economic sphere was one of the root causes of alienation under capitalism and that therefore, to achieve a non-alienated society, competition should be eliminated. Marxists who have turned their attention to sports have suggested the same solution in the sporting as in the economic sphere; the evils of athletic competition will only be eliminated with the elimination of competitive athletics itself.[11] No one can deny that there is a problem of alienation in competitive athletics today. Intimidation, cheating, the notorious use of "cheap shots" and the regular outbreak of fisticuffs are only the most manifest instances of the problem. We shall inquire into the connection between that alienation and athletic competition itself. Is the connection a causal one, as the Marxists assume ("competition causes alienation"), and if so, should we go along with their proposed solution? Or, *contra* the Marxists, is it the case that athletic competition *per se* is not the cause of alienation but that the connection is more complex? If so, what is that connection, and what should our response to it be? Again, we shall discover that competitive athletics offers us a focal case study for understanding the broader problematic of competition itself.

Chapter 3, "Sport and Self-Knowledge," turns attention to a set of issues under the loose heading of the "psychology of sport." One of the claims often made by the proponents of sport—and particularly by those who claim that sport has important educational value—is that through participation in sport we learn about ourselves, and so fulfill the age-old philosophic demand to "know thyself." We shall examine this claim in depth. What is it that we learn or can learn about our "self" in athletic competition, and what is the nature of that "self" about which we learn? These questions have been approached from a number of different perspectives, and we shall examine several. First will be a psychoanalytic perspective. Psychoanalysts such as Arnold Beisser have treated troubled athletes, and sought connections between their pathology and either their particular choices of sport, or the mode of involvement in the sport that they choose.[12] By looking at what we might call the categories of analysis Beisser employs, we shall consider to what extent these analytic categories can be helpful in informing us about the significance of our personal sport choices.

A second and very different claim to self-knowledge in sport has been set forth by various partisans of Zen Buddhism, who have found a rich field (in the financial as well as the intellectual sense!) of application in sport. Books entitled with some version of "Zen _____" (fill in the blank with your favorite sport) abound, but the best remains the one that fathered the others, Eugen Herrigel's *Zen in the Art of Archery*.[13] By examining the principles developed in that book, we shall consider to what extent "the Zen way" can be a path to self-knowledge through sport. Finally, we shall consider one of the oldest senses of self-knowledge, the Socratic one of "knowing what I know and what I do not know," and ask after the relevance of this sense of self-knowledge to the experience of sport.

Chapter 4, "Mind and Body in Sport," considers an issue related to the question of self-knowledge, the connection between mind and body, and how the sporting situation can shed light on this issue. The question of the connection of mind and body is, of course, an age-old one in philosophy. We can trace the straightforward dualism of the Pythagorean doctrine of reincarnation, through the Christian formulation of the immortality of the soul, to Descartes' dualism as asserted in his *Meditations on First Philosophy*. Countering what for a long time was this dominant dualist thesis are materialist or physicalist accounts which assert that there is no dualism of mind and body because "the mind" is really just part (albeit a very complex part) of the body. All is body. From a very different perspective, phenomenologists have also denied the efficacy of the mind/body separation, based not on materialist grounds but on experiential considerations. Their claim is that we simply do not experience such a distinction, that it is an intellectual abstraction which gets in the way of a genuine understanding of the human experience of oneself. Sporting activity, wherein the mind and the body are so actively engaged together, offers us a marvelous testing ground for the examination of this long-standing philosophic issue.

No one listens very long to discussions about sports without noticing the prevalence therein of the vocabulary of aesthetics. We hear of the beauty of a great runner's stride, the gracefulness of a basketball player's leap to the basket. Indeed, in some sports, such as diving, gymnastics, or equestrian sports, aesthetic criteria are actually used in determining the winner of the event. Accordingly, Chapter 5, "Sport, Art, and the Aesthetic," considers the nature of the connection between sport and art. The strongest claim made here is that sport, at least in its highest instances, is an art form, that the athlete—graceful, talented, creative—is a genuine artist. We shall consider the arguments for and against this claim. More cautious souls suggest that although there remain certain fundamental differences between art and sport, the deeply aesthetic character of many sports attests to a deep kinship between the two. What is the nature of that kinship? In particular, if sports are not straightforwardly art forms but nevertheless share a deep aesthetic component, what is the nature of that component which they share, and what are the important differences which finally distinguish sport and art? An examination of this set of questions hopefully will shed light both on the nature of sport and of art.

Finally, in Chapter 6, "The Stance of Sport," we shall try to gain a sense of "what's going on" when we play sports. What is our stance or orientation when we play and how does that stance differ from our more ordinary, everyday stances? Briefly, I shall suggest that when we play, we are called upon and call upon ourselves to be more open than we usually are, more aware of the possibilities that are presented to us and of what those possibilities signify. At the same time, we are also called upon to be more responsive to those possibilities as they arise, more capable of responding in a forceful and efficacious way so as to help determine the outcome of the game. "Responsive openness," then, will be our first version of what I call "the stance of play." But, as we shall discover, responsive openness by itself is hardly adequate to characterize our orientation when we play.

To fill out our understanding of that orientation which we call "playfulness," we shall consider a number of other important philosophic themes, which are especially manifest in our sporting play. For example, virtually every sport that we invent sets up an often arbitrary set of limitations within which the activity must remain: the spatial boundaries, the time limits, the rules of the game. In a life where we spend a good amount of time resisting the various limitations imposed upon us, what is the significance of the fact that in sport we freely choose to play within such limitations—that, as it were, we invite such confrontations with finitude?

This will lead us to a reflection on the human confrontation with finitude, how we attempt to transform limitation into possibility, and how sport offers us such a paradigmatic example of our attempt to do so. This in turn will help us to consider the decisive philosophic issue of human freedom as it is exhibited in sport, where we freely choose to enter into situations of sometimes radical finitude. We shall also look into the subtle place of "value" in sport, as well as the role of risk-taking and trust. Finally, but certainly not least important, we shall consider how and why the phenomenon of fun is such an integral aspect of our sport experience at its best.

A word may be appropriate at this point concerning the ordering of the chapters and the connections between them. On the one hand, each chapter is intended to stand by itself as an attempt to address some of the major issues in each of the designated areas. In theory, therefore, a reader particularly interested in the connection of sport and art should be able to benefit from Chapter 5 without reading the prior chapters. Nevertheless, there is a loose order to the chapters, beginning with what I take to be the most general and pervasive issue, sport and society, and moving gradually to increasingly specific areas. Thus, following the first chapter's treatment of themes in sport and society, the second chapter focuses more specifically on some of the important ethical issues that arise in and out of that relationship. Chapter 3, "Sport and Self-Knowledge," then moves from the interactive realm of ethics to the significance of sport for the individual athlete. Chapter 4, "Mind and Body in Sport," continues that theme by asking about the nature of that "individual" who might come to self-knowledge in sport. Chapter 5 then turns to a very specific aspect of sporting experience, its aesthetic component, and asks after the connection of sport and art. Finally, Chapter 6 returns to a synoptic standpoint by trying to reflect on what our stance of play is whenever we play any sport. Hopefully it will serve to tie the issues of the previous chapters together by understanding something of "what's going on" when we play.

Our consideration of these themes will hardly exhaust the philosophic issues present in sport. But this book will fulfill its purpose if it serves as an adequate introduction to some of the most important and enduring philosophic themes as they are exhibited in our sport experience. If, in so doing, a further step is taken toward establishing sporting experience as a legitimate and important realm for philosophic investigation, the book, at least in its author's mind, will be a resounding success.

NOTES

1. Huizinga, Johan, *Homo Ludens: A Study of the Play Element in Culture*. Boston, Beacon Press, 1950; Foreword.

2. Diogenes Laertius, *The Lives and Opinions of Eminent Philosophers*, translated by C. D. Yonge. London, Henry G. Bohn, 1853, page 65, 114.

3. Plato, *Republic*, 411e, ff.

4. Plato, *Laws*, 803c, ff.

5. Nietzsche, Friedrich, *Philosophy in the Tragic Age of the Greeks*, translated by Marianne Cowan. Chicago, Gateway Editions, 1962, page 62.

6. For a detailed discussion of this development, see Chapter 5 of my *The Question of Play*, Lanham, Md., University Press of America, 1984.

7. Sartre, Jean-Paul, *Being and Nothingness: An Essay on Phenomenological Ontology*, translated by Hazel Barnes. New York, Philosophical Library, 1956, page 580 ff.

8. Wittgenstein, Ludwig, *Philosophical Investigations*, translated by G.E.M. Anscombe. New York, MacMillan Company, 1953. Part I.

9. Herrigel, Eugen, *Zen in the Art of Archery*. New York, Vintage Books, 1971.

10. Weiss, Paul, *Sport: A Philosophic Inquiry*. Carbondale, Ill., Southern Illinois University Press, 1969.

11. See for example Brohm, Jean-Marie, *Sport: A Prison of Measured Time*, translated by Ian Fraser. London, Ink Links Press, 1978.

12. Beisser, Arnold, *The Madness in Sport*. Bowie, Md., Charles Press Publishers, 1977.

13. Herrigel, Eugen, *op. cit.*

CHAPTER ONE

SPORT
AND SOCIETY

As indicated in the introduction, sport plays a significant role in the cultural life of most societies. As Johan Huizinga has shown, this is true not only of more advanced modern societies, but even of ancient and primitive ones.[1] Nevertheless, one could plausibly speculate that it has never been more true than in contemporary American society. Millions of our citizens participate in competitive sports of one sort or another. Only a small minority of these participants play at the highly visible levels of professional, intercollegiate, or interscholastic sport. Although it is easy to overlook this fact, the vast majority of sports events take place at the "sand-lot" or informal level. In addition to actual participation, attendance at sporting events around the country probably exceeds a million spectators per week. If we add to that the even greater number of people who watch televised sports, we see that sports touch the lives of enormous numbers of people. Metaphors and the vocabulary of the sports world now pervade nearly every walk of life; presidents speak of cooperative cabinet members as "team players," and heavy investors in the stock market are called "major players." Clearly, then, sports constitutes an important cultural phenomenon. What are the major issues of philosophic interest present in this convergence of sporting and societal issues?

SPORT AND VALUES

The first theme we shall take up bears directly on this relationship. It is clear to nearly everyone that, in both the good and the bad senses, the values in sport are at least in part a reflection of the values of the society in which the sports take place. The 19th century philosopher Hegel suggested that we understand a people by the gods they worship; one could make a similar claim about the sports popular among a people. A sport culture which emphasizes such values as teamwork, self-discipline, willingness to sacrifice personal glory for the benefit of the team, or the importance of sustained training, clearly tells us something about the cultural values, the cultural needs, of the society in which those sports take place. But this is no less true if the sport values include unquestioning obedience to authority, willingness to hurt others in pursuit of a goal, to lie, cheat, intimidate, and to risk the ruin of one's physical health.

Once it is recognized that the values present in the sport world are a reflection of the values of society, it is a plausible inference that sports can and do teach those values to its participants. Given the intensity of involvement that many people experience in sport, together with the fact that most sports present us with a learning atmosphere in order that we may develop and perfect the skills relevant to the given sport, it is plausible enough to suppose that sports will also teach the values reflected in them. Enthusiasts who praise sports for their capacity to teach the values of teamwork, self-discipline, and fair play, invariably appeal to the promise that those values, learned in a sporting context, will be useful, perhaps even more useful, in the context of life itself. General Douglas MacArthur is reported to have said that "On the friendly fields of athletic strife are sown the seeds which, on other days, on other fields, will reap the fruits of victory." To say this is to recognize both that sports do teach those values and that those values are not peculiar to sport but relevant and necessary to life in general.

Perhaps the strongest claim of this sort was made by the French writer Albert Camus, who once claimed that the only situation where he ever really learned ethics was in sport.[2]

The order of movement here seems to be as follows: First, sports are a reflection of the values inherent in a given society. That is, the values originate in the society at large, and are then reflected in the sports that that society generates. With a slightly different emphasis, the values that sports exhibit are not inherent in sport as sport, but are reflections of values that originate in society. But second, sports *teach* those values, instill them in the participants so that, in turn, those values, learned in the sporting context, are carried back into the society from which they originate. It is on the assumption of this structure that sports are so often praised for the values they can teach.

The exact same structure is assumed by the harshest critics of competitive sport. The difference is that such critics see a very different set of values being reflected and passed along by sport. Because of its clarity and forthrightness, I shall concentrate on the Marxian critique of competitive sport, but as I hope will be clear, such a critique has come to be largely shared by "liberal" critics of sport as well.

In order to better understand this critique, it may be helpful to set out, if only in outline, certain elements of the Marxian critique of capitalism. According to this analysis, capitalism is a developmental stage in world economy which begins in the quasi-primitive situation of scarcity. At some very early point in human social development, we were faced with a situation where there was not a sufficient supply of the basic needs—food, clothing, and shelter—to go around. This engendered what we might call the primal situation of competition. Two things should be noted about this original condition: First, it was brought about by economic conditions—the scarcity of basic needs—and thus is not, according to the Marxian analysis, a "natural" condition of human beings. As such, given the right conditions—the abolition of scarcity—competition could presumably be abolished. Second, the conditions under which this competition takes place are inherently alienating. This is a struggle for survival itself; under these conditions, it is absurd to ask for friendship and fair play among the competitors. People struggling for survival under conditions of scarcity where only some will live inevitably will be alienated from one another.

The first economic response to this was the ingenious solution of the division of labor. By assigning different tasks to different people with different abilities (the shoemaker only makes shoes, the farmer only grows crops, etc.), it was plausibly supposed that a much greater quantity of the goods needed could be produced, and scarcity could be overcome. Unfortunately, things were not that simple. The division of labor turned out to exacerbate the problem of competition, because certain occupations came to have a controlling power over others. The economic divisions between what quickly became the rich and the poor grew even more acute, and with it the accompanying alienation.

To make a very long story short, capitalism does not reach its full flowering until the industrial revolution and the development of the means of mass production through modern industry. At this point, according to Marx, capitalism reaches a new stage. For now, thanks to the development of modern industry, we have in principle the means to overcome scarcity. Given the development of industry in the 19th century, Marx was confident that if our productive capacities were properly organized, if we made socially beneficial products, and if goods were fairly distributed, it would be possible to satisfy people's needs. The problem, or, to use Marxian terminology, the contradiction, is that the very system—capitalism, which allows in principle for the overcoming of scarcity—will in fact never bring it about. This is because of certain characteristics of the system itself, to wit, competition and what follows from a competitive framework: alienation, greed, and a lack of concern for one's fellow humans.

In its developed form, capitalism, or to be more precise, the competition inherent in capitalism, brings about alienation in four ways.[3] First, the worker experiences alienation from the product he or she makes. A worker in a Cadillac assembly line, for example, puts creative energy—sometimes exhausting creative energy—into a product that not only could he or she not afford to buy, but which, in the possession of those who can afford it, will be held over against the worker as a sign of the automobile owner's "superiority" to the worker. The very product of the worker's creative energy thus gets turned against him or her, and alienation results.

This leads directly to the second form of alienation, self-alienation. The worker's own creative energy, as the above example attests, gets turned against the worker. Since, according to Marx, human beings are essentially creative or productive beings (*Homo faber*), alienation from the product of that creative impulse is tantamount to alienation from oneself. The worker sees the product of his own work turned against him or her, and experiences self-alienation.

But since this creative, productive activity is, according to Marx, not just a contingent characteristic but the very essence of human nature, what Marx calls "species being,"[4] such alienation, thirdly, is at once alienation from human nature itself. From this, fourthly and inevitably, follows alienation from one's fellow humans, both from the owners who oppress the worker and from the fellow workers with whom, given the system of capitalism, one is forced to compete for one's very survival.

This brief summary of the Marxist critique of alienation under capitalism should enable us to understand how it gets plausibly applied to competition in sport. First, we are told, sports clearly reflect the values of the society in which they arise. In this case, all the worst values of capitalism are reflected in competitive sport. The alienation supposedly endemic to capitalist competition, its concomitant values of winning at all costs, self-degradation in the name of "beating" someone, mindless obedience to authority, willingness to hurt others, all these values present in sport are but reflections of the worst of capitalism's values. As the French Marxist Jean-Marie Brohm puts it,

Sport. . . . contains all the values of traditional, repressive morality and hence all the models of behavior promoted by bourgeois society: the cult of duty for its own sake, the sense of sacrifice for the community, the ideology of the super-ego, obedience, discipline, etc.[5]

Moreover, sport values are not simply reflections of capitalist values; sports teaches those values as well.

Firstly, sport trains the work force to operate according to the norms of capitalist, or bureaucratic state-capitalist exploitation. Sport is basically a mechanisation of the body, treated as an automaton, governed by the principle of maximising output.[6]

One need not be a Marxist to appreciate the general force of Brohm's argument. If the values in sport are reflections of the values of society and sports teaches those values, and if, in addition, those values are undesirable, then we have a serious problem with sport. Moreover, even advocates of the potentially positive value of sport (among whom I count myself) must surely admit that there *are* undesirable values often inculcated by sport, particularly by misguided coaches.[7] We need not adhere to the Marxian solution that "Sport is alienating. It will disappear in a universal communist society,"[8] to agree that we do indeed have a problem.

As the above quote attests, the Marxian critique of sport is founded on the argument, crucial to their analysis of capitalism, that competition is inherently alienating, that competition is an essential and irreducible component of capitalism, and therefore that to get rid of alienation one must abolish capitalism. On this argument, the competitive aspect of sport makes it inherently alienating. There is no way to "save" competitive sport from its alienating consequences, and the only way to resolve the problem is to abolish competitive sport. In a later chapter, we shall return to the issue of whether the connection between alienation and athletic competition is necessary or contingent. If we discover that competition in sport is indeed inherently alienating, the Marxian analysis will have clear applicability to sport. If, on the other hand, we discover that the connection between competitive sport and alienation is only a contingent one—that sport can be alienating but does not have to be—we shall want to modify the Marxian analysis in significant ways.

The Marxian critique of competitive sport and its relation to societal values is a challenging one, but it is certainly not the only one. One could argue, for example, that it is not competition or anything else *inherent* in sport that is undercutting its value. Rather, other values in society, values not at all intrinsic to sport itself, are being imported into sport to its detriment. Christopher Lasch, for example, argues that contemporary sport is being degraded and trivialized precisely by being turned into a vehicle for education, the enhancement of business, and entertainment.[9] Sports, he suggests, in principle constitute their own "culture," which is in fundamental ways independent of the larger culture out of which they arise. Sports

. . . enlist skill and intelligence, the utmost concentration of purpose, on behalf of activities utterly useless, which make no contribution to the struggle of man against nature, to the wealth or comfort of the community, or to its physical survival.[10]

Nevertheless, sports do bear a certain connection to the surrounding culture in that they

. . . offer a dramatic commentary on reality rather than an escape from it—a heightened reenactment of communal traditions, not a repudiation of them.[11]

Lasch argues that this delicate balance—that sport both reflects societal values yet constitutes an independent culture—is ruined when sport is "forced into the service of education, character development, or social improvement."[12] This degradation becomes complete as sport has become a big business and part of the entertainment industry. The way to restore sport to its health would be (if this were possible) to relieve it of the business, entertainment, and educational burdens imposed upon it and restore it to its own integrity.

Note that Lasch's analysis still preserves the connection between sport and society, set out above: that the values in sport derive from and are a reflection of those in society. But unlike the Marxists, Lasch's is an example of a critique of sport that suggests that those negative values instilled in sport from society are contingent to sport itself. They could in principle be eliminated from sport (though Lasch himself does not seem especially optimistic about this). Sport thus would be liberated from the incursion into it of values from society that undercut its true nature.

For our purposes, it is important to recognize that the Marxian and Laschian analyses are examples of two ways that one might view the connection of sport and society critically. The Marxian analysis presents a structure in which the values inherent in sport are indeed reflections of the values inherent in society (in this case, the negative values of capitalism), but that those values are so deeply a part of competitive sport that they become constitutive of sport itself. As such, the only way to eliminate the defects is to eliminate competitive sport, at least as it presently exists. In this sense, it is a more "radical" critique than the one exemplified by Lasch. He claims that at present, sport is affected to its detriment by certain values derived from society. But since these values are not inherent to sport itself, they could in principle be eliminated from sport, thus not only preserving but enhancing sport itself. If one holds to a critique such as this, one will advocate not the elimination but the "reform" of sport. Nevertheless, both critiques assume the two premises discussed so far, that the values in sport are a reflection of those in society, and that sports teach those values.

It should be noted that a third, implicit premise in these arguments is that the values in sport somehow all originate in society. To put the point somewhat differently, sport has no inherent or intrinsic values of its own—values, for example, that might be carried into society to the latter's benefit. There is, it should be noted, an implicit hint at this latter possibility in Lasch's claim that the values of sport cannot be completely assimilated to those of society. In an instructive remark, Lasch says,

Sport does play a role in socialization, but the lessons it teaches are not necessarily the ones that coaches and teachers of physical education seek to impart. The mirror theory of sport (that the values in sport mirror those of society), like all reductionist interpretations of culture, makes no allowance for the autonomy of cultural traditions. In sport, these traditions come down from one generation of players to another, and although athletics do reflect social values, they can never be completely assimilated to those values.[13]

If this is so, we might allow for the possibility that sport might contain some values which are not merely derived from society, values which might even be subversive to those of society, or values which might beneficially be carried back into society. We can raise and perhaps shed light on this possibility by turning our attention to two issues that are obviously serious problems in our society and have been no less so in sport: racism and sexism.

RACISM IN SPORT

Let us begin with racism. The manifest presence of racism in sport is a perfect instance of the claim that the values of a given society will be reflected in its sporting institutions. In its "purer" forms, when segregation was a formal institution in the country as a whole, blacks were segregated from most of the major sports and had to form their own leagues. When segregation was outlawed, we learned to our dismay that that was hardly the end to racism; its form simply became more subtle, more sophisticated, and in many ways more insidious. The same pattern occurred in organized sport. After segregation was banned, blacks were gradually integrated into organized sport, but often with strict, if unstated, quotas. Bill Russell, the great Boston Celtic center, is said to have claimed that in the early days of integrated basketball, teams would "start two blacks at home, three on the road, and four when they had to win." Moreover, even after formal integration, blacks were for a long time excluded from certain key "skill" positions, such as quarterback in football. Even today, there is much controversy about the stunning paucity of blacks in the coaching and management positions of professional sport.

Few would deny that important steps have been taken in the last thirty years or so to overcome racism in our society. But few would deny as well that racism still remains a problem, a problem in some ways more insidious because it is for the most part less straightforward, outspoken, and "honest." Thus the complaints of some whites that blacks and other minorities should be "satisfied" with the progress that has been made are insensitive to the more subtle but no less powerful and painful ways in which racism still holds sway.

Again, we find the same syndrome present in the world of sport. One example of a more subtle form of racism present in sport today concerns the assessment of great athletes and how they achieve their prowess. White athletes who attain "superstar" status are invariably praised for the hard work, commitment, sacrifice, etc., that they must exhibit to achieve their excellence. Black superstars, on the other hand, are often characterized as "natural" athletes. The claim implicit in this apparently innocent epithet is that they did not have to exhibit the virtues of hard work and commitment that the white stars did—after all, blacks are just naturally gifted. It is understandable that black athletes, who have worked just as hard, just as long, and made just as many sacrifices as their white counterparts, would be irritated at the subtle racism exhibited in these judgments.

Considerations such as these make clear the plausibility of the claim that there has been and still is racism present in sport, and that this racism is a reflection of the racism still present in our society. The alternative would seem to be to argue that sports themselves are somehow *inherently* racist, that there is something racist about the *nature* of, say, baseball, or tennis, or golf. I have yet to discover anyone who suggested that. But that is to say that racism is not a necessary but a contingent characteristic of sport. Surely, most of us could agree that racism in principle could be eliminated from sports, and they would still be the sports that they are—indeed, they would be superior in their reformed state.

If racism, like so many of the "values" in sport, is derived from society and is a contingent characteristic of sports themselves, then it raises the question broached earlier: Are there other values "intrinsic" to the sporting situation—values which might even be carried into society to its benefit? Let me try to make that possibility plausible with the example of racism. Imagine yourself at a playground basketball court. You know that the conventions of the court are that the winning team gets to keep on playing, while the losing team must sit until their next turn comes around. Imagine as well that this is a popular court with a large number of participants waiting to play, so that losing the game will more or less assure that you will be sitting for an hour or two. Typically for a sporting situation, this puts a considerable stake on winning. Now imagine further that the teams are being picked. You are one of those choosing sides. You happen to be white. Obviously, you want to pick the best team possible so as to maximize your chances of continuing to play. The best player waiting to be chosen when your turn comes is black. But you are racist; you much prefer not to have blacks on your team. So you pass over the superior black player to choose an inferior player, but one who is white. In this situation, the preservation of your racism has a clear price, the likelihood that you will lose and have to sit.

A closer look at this fairly typical athletic situation suggests that the very structure of the situation—the choosing of sides and a clear stake in winning—carries implicit in it a set of values, or at least, quite clear lessons. For example, one maximizes one's chances of doing well if one acts according to the following principle: "Judge people according to their ability." (In this example, their basketball ability, but the principle is obviously transferable.) If one takes this principle to heart more generally, it might be a small step toward the overcoming of racism.[14]

I use this example to be suggestive of a possibility, that the "direction" of movement between values in society and sport might be two ways, that while it is certainly true that certain values exhibited in sports are reflections of those same values originating in society (the case of racism), there might be other values intrinsic to the very structure of the sporting situation itself, values which one might want to see reflected in the society at large.

In my own youth, before the civil rights movement got into full swing, I can recall occasionally hearing, as "justification" for the segregation of blacks in organized sport, the claim that they were simply inferior athletes and it would be humiliating for them to compete with whites. A few years later, after it was demonstrated that they were at least as capable athletes as whites, one began to hear a perverse version of the exact opposite argument, that the reason blacks were "superior" athletes was that they were genetically and physiologically closer to primitive conditions where athletic prowess was necessary for survival. The former argument, asserting the inferiority of blacks as athletes, was no doubt in "bad faith" from the beginning, and in retrospect I suspect that even its proponents probably did not fully believe it. The latter argument, however, is still controversial today. It is no longer used as a justification for separation of whites and minorities in sport but as an explanation for the remarkable success of minorities, especially blacks, in American athletics.

Surely, something about the situation does call for explanation. For example, 75 percent of the basketball players in the NBA are black, as are 55 percent of the football players in the NFL. Especially given the fact that in the nation at large blacks still represent a small minority of the total population, these figures attest to a stunning level of athletic achievement by blacks. How are we to explain this? The first thing that needs to be said is that no one knows. An adequate explanation of this phenomenon is yet to be presented. Moreover, the problem is exacerbated by the sensitivity of race relations, which is the context for such an investigation. Often the very effort to investigate the question is regarded as a sign of implicit racism, particularly for those who wish to investigate the possibility of genetic or physiological differences.

Nevertheless, two general directions of explanation are discernible: sociological explanations and genetic or physiological explanations. The sociological explanations, which seem to be predominant at present, base their account on an interpretation of the sociological differences that typify the childhood and nurturing of white and black youth. Perhaps the most common version of this account points to the lower socioeconomic status of most blacks as the basis of an explanation. Faced with a struggle for survival throughout their lives, blacks earlier and more readily develop the competitive attitude which, turned to the athletic realm, helps make them superior athletes. Conversely, many white youths, by contrast, "have it too easy" to become great athletes. Or alternatively, blacks, faced with de facto exclusion from many of the standard paths to economic success, recognize early on that athletic success is one of the few avenues to financial success genuinely open to them (the "way out of the ghetto" argument).

Either of these arguments, or variants of them, appeal not to anything inherently or "naturally" different about blacks which would make them superior athletes but to the socio-economic conditions under which they are raised. One appeal of this explanation is that in denying any "natural" differences relevant to athletic success, it avoids establishing an explanatory framework—"whites and blacks are just different"—which has been at the ideological foundation of so much of racism.

The second explanatory framework, genetic or physiological explanation, is for that very reason much more controversial. Here the explanation of enormous athletic success among blacks takes some form of the claim that genetic or physiological differences between blacks and whites predispose them to athletic prowess. Claims have been made, for example, about differences in muscle fiber, about statistical differences in muscle configuration, and even, at the level of silliness, that blacks have an extra bone in their foot, the latter used as an explanation of why so many black basketball players are outstanding leapers. Although fortunately few are given to explanations such as the latter, the phenomenon it seeks to explain, the remarkable leaping ability of many black athletes, is widely enough accepted that even among blacks, the occasional black athlete who does not jump especially well is characterized as suffering from "white man's disease."

Even the serious investigations into possible genetic or physiological differences are controversial both scientifically and politically. They are controversial scientifically because the evidence supporting or denying the claim that biological differences might explain differences in athletic prowess is not strong enough to be widely accepted. Indeed, whether or not there even are objectively delineable racial characteristics is itself controversial. It may be, for example, that the differences between skin pigmentation or facial structure from, say, Swedes to Zulus, simply reflect a range or spectrum, and no more constitute evidence for "objective" differences in race than would the difference between people under five feet tall and people over seven feet. Perhaps the former range of difference has simply been invested with a political significance that the latter does not have.[15]

But such scientific investigations are also controversial politically. We know from bitter experience in the past that claims about the "natural inferiority" of blacks have been used as part of the ideological basis for racism and the systematic exclusion of blacks from conventional avenues to social and economic success. Now, ironically, converse hypotheses about the natural superiority of blacks as athletes are being entertained. Many fear that, in the context of a still racist society, arguments about natural differences between races, even if ostensibly pointing to the superiority of blacks, will nevertheless be put in the ideological service of racism. Indeed, there is already some evidence that this fear is warranted. As mentioned in an earlier discussion, the claim that blacks are "natural" athletes has ironically been turned against them as implicit or explicit evidence that they do not need to exhibit, and therefore need not be praised for, such virtues as discipline, commitment, and sustained effort for which white athletes are regularly praised.

Another version of this ironic transformation of black athletic superiority into the service of racism plays on the well-known dualism of mind and body. Yes, the claim goes, blacks are naturally superior athletes. But the inference drawn from this is that they are therefore probably inferior intellectually. White players, having to overcome their supposedly inferior natural ability, do so, it is suggested, by being "smart" players, by "knowing the game" so well, by being "heady." The inference is easily (if implicitly) drawn that when black players accomplish the same feats as whites, it is by virtue not of their intelligence but of their "natural ability." However absurd the conclusion, it is so often drawn that black athletes, sensitive to these implications, have found themselves moved to deny characterizations of their "natural" ability ostensibly intended as praise.

This situation puts contemporary scientists interested in

investigating this issue in a difficult, delicate, but not unprecedented position. On the one hand, next to none of them, hopefully, wants the results of their investigations put in the service of racism. On the other hand, should they hold back their conclusions or even hold back from investigating these issues on the grounds that the results might be controversial or politically "dangerous?" Most researchers, deeply committed to freedom of inquiry and some version or other of the enlightenment conviction that "the truth shall make you free," resist the latter path as a dire threat to academic freedom and to science itself. Nevertheless, it is with understandable fear and trembling that a scientist of good will would embark on an investigation the results of which might be put to deplorable uses.

In the investigation of the statistically enormous athletic success of blacks, then, we have an issue which is intellectually fascinating, potentially important to our understanding of human beings, yet politically delicate and even dangerous. It will be interesting to watch what happens with this issue in the coming years.

SEXISM IN SPORT

A controversy similar in many ways to the problem of racism in sport exists when we turn to sexism. For years and even centuries, women have been systematically excluded from full participation in sport. The evidence for this claim is painfully obvious, from the relatively small participation in sport among women, to the amount of money spent on women's sports, to the extent of press coverage of women's athletics, even to the different ways in which little girls are raised. What is more controversial, again, is the explanation of this phenomenon. Is it straightforwardly the result of sexism in society? That is, is it simply a social phenomenon which, as such, could be overcome in a more just society? Or are there reasons and even justifications for the exclusion of women from full participation in sport?

In this case too, a number of accounts for the phenomenon have gained some acceptance. One view argues that however equal women might be to men intellectually, women are simply and clearly weaker and smaller than men physically, and therefore naturally inferior as athletes. Given the clear statistical differences in size, in ratios of fat to muscle, even in muscle and bone structure, women simply do not have the physical ability to compete with men as athletes, and they should not try, or so the argument goes.[16]

To this is added a second argument, based on the "values" supposedly inculcated in our youth through participation in sport. It has been asserted that such values as discipline, competitiveness, courage, and indeed "manliness" are most desirable for our male youth to develop—hence the value of sports participation for them—but that such values are unnecessary and even detrimental to the presumably different "nature" of women. A stunning example of this argument was made in the early seventies in Connecticut. A female high school runner, manifestly superior to her female peers, sought more adequate competition by going out for the boys' track team. She was refused the opportunity and challenged the case in court. The judge, deciding against her, affirmed that "Athletic competition builds character in our boys. We do not need that kind of character in our girls."[17]

Such a claim may bring derisive laughter or righteous indignation to most of us today, but we should not dismiss it. For it hides a claim that is in principle important; not merely are there physical differences between women and men which militate against the full participation of women in athletics, there are intellectual, moral, or spiritual differences as well. Women and men are physically and spiritually different, and those differences make a difference when it comes to the appropriateness of athletic competition. This is the clear presumption of the judge's argument.

A different argument, still based upon the presumed difference between male and female nature, has been offered by Paul Weiss in his ground-breaking book on the philosophy of sport.[18] Weiss argues that one of the things that sport accomplishes is to overcome the experienced separation between mind and body that so many men experience. Because sport demands both physical and mental activity, and because one invests one's entire being, mental and physical in it, it offers us one of the few occasions for bridging the gap between the mind and the body—so typical of men's experience of things. But, Weiss argues, this diremption is peculiar to men. Women, thanks to childbirth, their supposedly more emotional natures, and even their menstrual cycle, are so naturally in touch with their bodies that they do not experience a diremption between mind and body and so do not need sport to overcome it. Sport is therefore appealing and valuable to men and more or less useless to women because it answers to a problem—the separation of mind and body—that men suffer but women simply do not have.

Such arguments, it should be noted, are founded on a claimed difference in the natures of women and men, either physical differences or spiritual and moral differences. They are proffered as reasons why women do not excel in sports, are less interested in sports than men, or as justifications for the exclusion of women from sport.

In recent years, however, such arguments have come under attack, both empirically and philosophically. The empirical evidence is all around us, in the enormous increase in participation of women in sport, in the clear satisfaction they get from sport, and perhaps most significantly, in the sometimes astonishing improvement in women's athletic achievement. The tennis courts, the softball diamonds, road races, and fitness centers are increasingly full of women just as committed as the men to the sport of their choice. Once given the opportunity, it is clear that the significance, satisfaction, and depth of involvement of women in sport can equal that of men. It is also clear that their poorer record of achievement relative to men in sport in the past was more a function of women's exclusion from adequate opportunities to develop and train than to inherent physical differences. Now that opportunities to train and learn are increasing for women, so too are their standards of achievement.

It is often pointed out, for example, that the times in women's Olympic swimming races would have been sufficient to win the men's events only a few years ago. Women's basketball players are now developing their strength so that some of them can even dunk. Indeed, in some sports particularly adapted to women's physiology, such as ultra-marathoning, it is predicted that in a few years women's times will be better than men's. All this offers evidence that a significant part of the explanation for women's relative inadequacy at sport in the past was that they were systematically excluded from the training and development opportunities which would have allowed them to excel.

Philosophically as well, a number of arguments have been put forward recently that call into question whatever justifications might have been offered in the past for the exclusion of women from sport. The first begins by noticing that the vast majority of our sports, and certainly all the "big-time" ones, have been developed by men and designed to showcase those qualities particularly characteristic of male musculature and body type: strength, speed, and size. Given that "bias" of most sports, it is hardly surprising that women have not excelled as much as men at sports which, after all, were not even developed for their body types. Some thinkers, Betsy Postow, for example, argue that given this built-in bias for most of our sports, it is dubious wisdom for women to actively participate in those very activities in which they are bound to "look bad" compared to men.[19] Why should women play basketball, for example, a sport consummately developed to highlight height, speed, and strength, the very qualities that on the whole will be exhibited to a greater extent by men? Instead, women should concentrate on sports specifically designed to highlight their own physiological tendencies, such as the balance beam in gymnastics, diving, or ultra-marathoning. Moreover, since, given the enormous domination of sport by males, the vast majority of sports are not designed for women, women should demand that more such sports be developed and take an active role in developing them.

This argument is sometimes countered by asking why women should deny themselves the opportunity to play, say, basketball (and the fun of so playing), just because on balance they will not be as big or fast as their male counterparts? The sex-differences, it is argued, are perhaps a justification for separating the men's and women's games in the name of fairness, but surely not for excluding women. Moreover, from a spectator standpoint, games between well-matched women's teams can be as exciting as those between men. In some sports, such as tennis, many consider the women's matches to be in fact even more exciting since they are not so dominated by power serves. Still, the point is well-taken that the bias against women in sport is already built into the very structure of most of our games, and surely something could and should be done about that.

A second argument, put forward by the philosopher Iris Marion Young, focuses its attack directly on the injustice of the exclusion of women from sport.[20] Young begins with the distinction between the experience of oneself—or others—as "body-subject" and as "body-object." To experience oneself as body-subject is to experience oneself as a source of activity, energy, and power. To experience oneself or others as body-object is to experience one as a thing, as passive, as something to be looked at, and decisively, as "the other." Once this distinction is established, Young can argue plausibly for a number of claims. First, sport is a paradigm realm of the body-subject.

The identity of body and active subjectivity reaches its paradigm in sport; the very stance, muscles, movement, and directionality of the athlete exhibit directly her or his intentions and projects. . . . sport calls upon the body's capacities and skills merely for the sake of determining what they can achieve. By its nature, then, sport exhibits the essential body-subject.[21]

Young's second claim, however, is that our culture, dominated by the masculine, has largely identified the body-subject, source of energy, activity, power, as the domain of the masculine. Conversely, it has identified body-object, entity to be looked at, passive, other, as the essence of the feminine. The force of this association will, I hope, be immediately plausible. In an all-too-common cultural scenario, while little boys are out on the athletic fields learning to be active, energetic, and assertive, little girls are at home learning to "primp" and "be beautiful." Or again, in discussions with my classes on the topic, I have discovered that for the most part male students, though they may joke about it, simply do not know what it really means to be taken as a "sex-object," and for a very good reason: it has simply never happened to them. But to the women it is all too familiar.

Given the body-subjective character of sport and the cultural associations of men with body-subjectivity and women as body-objects, Young's third claim becomes clear, that women have been not only "existentially" but conceptually excluded from sport. That is, in our very conception of what women are, we fundamentally exclude them from the realm of sport. But this is to exclude them from a realm of essential humanity. As Young points out, it is thus an injustice both to women and to sport, which is itself excluded from the full richness of the potential contribution of women.

Young's argument is a forceful one. Sport is indeed one of the decisive realms—and especially in our youth—where we experience ourselves as sources of energy, of power, of creative and self-creating activity. To exclude women from that possibility is to exclude them from an important, even definitive possibility of development. It has obviously contributed to their identification and, as Young points out, even their self-identification, as "sex-objects."[22] And just as obviously, justice demands that this exclusion be overcome.

A third argument is one I have championed in an article entitled "Competition, Friendship, and Human Nature."[23] It focuses not so much on the question of the relative athletic abilities of men and women as on the question of whether the various values proclaimed for sports are as appropriate for women as men. That is, in contrast to the judge quoted earlier, are sports as "good" for our little girls as for our little boys? I argue that they are.

A distinction can be drawn between claims regarding the natural physiological differences between men and women, about which there is relatively little controversy, and the question of whether there are natural (as opposed to culturally determined) psychological, intellectual, or "spiritual" differences. About the physiological differences between men and women—our "plumbing," musculature, differences in size and strength over a statistical range, etc.—there is some controversy but relatively little. Some might argue, for example, that at least some of the difference in size or strength or muscle development might be the result of social conditioning—how boys and girls are raised, the extent to which they are encouraged to be active, etc.—rather than "natural," genetically determined differences. Nevertheless, few would deny the reality of at least some natural genetic or physiological differences.

When we turn to the question of psychological, intellectual, or spiritual differences, however, the situation is altogether more murky. To be sure, differences at this level between men and women, at least across large samplings, seem to be discernible: the tendency for men to be more aggressive, for women to be more at ease with the expression of their emotions, more gentle, more "intuitive," etc. What is exceedingly difficult to determine is whether those perceived tendencies are the result of social conditioning or are "natural," that is, again, genetically determined differences independent of the way in which one is raised. This is both an important issue and a controversial one, and it has certainly not been definitively answered.

Whatever the nature of these differences, it should not be forgotten that there is another level of our natures which men and women share as human—what has for centuries been discussed as the question of "human nature." Again, just what that human nature is, or even whether such a nature is "permanent" or itself historically conditioned, is an immensely difficult and important issue. What we need to appreciate for the question of sports participation is that there are at least some characteristics, both physical and spiritual, which men and women will share by virtue of being human.

My point in raising these distinctions is not to claim a solution but to enable me to ask a different question which may be answerable. Whatever the differences between men and women and whatever their origin, does the difference make a difference when it comes to the supposed values derived from sport? Keep in mind that those characteristics which sports are claimed to inculcate include both bodily and spiritual values. Sports, it is claimed, develop strong bodies, good health, agility, but also self-confidence, self-discipline, teamwork, competitive spirit, and the spirit of fair play.

The question, then, is this: Whatever the differences between men and women, whether it be the physiological differences or the more controversial spiritual ones, do those differences have any affect on the appropriateness of the various values derived from sport? If there are values derived from sports participation which are a function of some of the differences between men and women, to that extent the judge may be right that such values and sports may be appropriate for men and inappropriate or irrelevant to women. That is what the judge claims, and that is what, in a very different way, Paul Weiss had claimed. If, on the other hand, the values available in sport are a function not of differences in our nature but of characteristics which women and men share as human, then the value of sport is as relevant to women as men, and the massive exclusion of women from the opportunity to share and enjoy those values is a manifest injustice.

This sets the framework for responding to the question of whether sport is an appropriate activity for women as well as men. We must look at the values supposedly available in sport and ask whether those values are related to aspects of our natures which are sexually differentiated—in which case, the difference will make a difference. Or are they rather connected to aspects of our natures as human in which case, we shall judge sport a humanly good thing rather than a "masculinely" good thing?

I shall not claim to develop a comprehensive list of all the values, physical and spiritual, available in sport. That is not necessary to establish the thrust of my argument, which is that surely most of the values claimed on behalf of sports participation are values appropriate to our natures as human rather than as male or female.

Begin with the physical values. Sport encourages health, strength, agility (although more than one skeptic has suggested that an intense involvement in sport, with its likely injuries, over-training, etc. is more likely to destroy one's physical health than to enhance it).[24] Granting the physical differences in general between women and men, even granting, for example, that women are typically not as strong as men, does that suggest that they should not be as strong as they could be, as agile as they could be, as healthy as they can be? Surely they should. If sport does encourage those traits, clearly sport is of value for women as well as men.

A similar argument holds true for what I have been calling the spiritual values. Take the ones mentioned just above: self-confidence, self-discipline, teamwork, competitive spirit, the spirit of fair play. In order to claim that participation in sport was somehow inappropriate for women, one would need to argue that somehow those values are inappropriate or irrelevant to women. I submit that one would have to be a male chauvinist of monumental proportions to claim that women do not need those qualities, or will not benefit from those qualities, as much as men.

Perhaps the most interesting issue here is the question of competitive spirit. One might question first whether the inculcation of competitive spirit is even desirable. We saw, for example, that the Marxian critique of sport is founded precisely on its inculcation of the deplorable trait of competitiveness. But note that nothing in Marx's critique suggests that competition is bad for men, or that it must be overcome among men. If competition is bad, it is bad for humans as human. Does not the converse hold, that if competitive spirit is a positive value, it is so for humans, not for men or women alone?

On the other hand, one might argue that insofar as competitive spirit is connected to aggressiveness, and insofar as aggressiveness is a predominantly male trait, competitiveness, and so the value of competitive sport, is, after all, gender specific. But this argument would depend on showing that competitive spirit is a desirable characteristic for men but not for women. Even if it were shown that men had a tendency to be more competitive than women (and the evidence for this is by no means conclusive), the analogy with physical strength suggests that it would still be valuable for women, even granting their "less competitive natures," to hone what competitive spirit they have in the proper way—supposedly the virtue of sport participation. And in any case, as I argue at length elsewhere, it is at least as likely that the competitive urge derives from something about our nature as human rather than our natures as male or female.[25] One way or another, then, the evidence seems to me conclusive that the desirable values present in sport are values to and for human beings and therefore should be available to all human beings. The value of sport, in that sense, is androgynous.

THE ATHLETE AS HERO

The final issue focusing primarily on sport and society to which I wish to turn is that of the sports hero. If a culture's heroes are its secular gods, one learns much about a culture by noting what qualities and personality types it elevates to hero-status. Presumably, a culture's heroes will exhibit those traits of character and personality that are most needful, most desirable, most honored in that culture. To take an obvious example, a culture whose heroes are predominantly warriors would attest to the need in that culture for warrior virtues: courage, aggressiveness, etc. We could predict that that culture existed in a politically precarious environment, one in which war was always a possibility, and therefore the virtues of warriors always needful.

In this sense, the oft-noted tendency for Americans to elevate its great athletes to hero status is thought-provoking and puzzling. We live, after all, in an epoch increasingly dominated by technology. One of the characteristics of technology is that it accomplishes by machinery more and more of the activities which once required the physical strength and agility of humans. Even war, once the special domain of the physically strong and courageous, has become increasingly an activity requiring more technological knowledge than physical strength. In a culture, then, in which physical strength and agility is less and less necessary for everyday life, why should we be elevating to hero status people whose activity exhibits just those increasingly anachronistic virtues?

One argument is that it is precisely the increasingly less practical character of the athlete's virtues that leads us to so admire our athletes. Athletes remind us of "the way we were"; they exhibit those qualities of physical strength, agility, and dexterity, which we all once needed in some form or other to go about our daily lives, but now typically neither need nor any longer exhibit. The hero status of athletes is thus a nostalgia for the past.

In its most negative version, this argument suggests that the athletic body has become like an orchid. It is a showy but useless spectacle which we may admire and may even goggle at, but which masks a fundamental pointlessness and sterility.[26] A more positive formulation of the point would be that we recognize in the athlete qualities that we are indeed in danger of losing, and that we want to preserve. The appeal of sport generally is thus in part the desire to find a way of preserving our bodily agility in an age in which such agility is in danger of atrophy. Athletes thus become our model—less for the way we were as the way we want to be—in spite of a technological culture which renders that way of being increasingly less "practical."

On the other hand, part of the appeal of athletes might have less to do with physical prowess than their other qualities. If what the proponents of athletics say is true, that sports does indeed embody and inculcate virtues that, far from useless, are most needful in our lives—qualities such as self-discipline, teamwork, etc.—then athletes may appeal to us insofar as they are literally the most visible exhibiters of those qualities. One sees the teamwork, self-discipline, concentration of the athlete in a way which is simply not as manifest for the businessman in his office, or the doctor in her hospital. On this argument, it is not only the physical but also the spiritual qualities which the athletes exhibit that leads us to admire them so.

Moreover, as Paul Weiss has observed, the athletic field is one of the first arenas where our youth can hope to achieve and exhibit the excellence that they admire in their athletic heroes. Long before a young person is capable of achieving excellence in business, politics, or ethics, he or she can achieve excellence in athletics.[27] That, surely, is part of its appeal, and part of the appeal of its outstanding example, the athletic hero.

Whatever the explanation of its source, this admiration is at times problematic. However admirable and worthy of imitation their athletic ability, great athletes sometimes lead ethical and moral lives which we would deplore. From Babe Ruth to Wade Boggs, from Joe Namath to Lawrence Taylor, athletes, even the greatest of them, have conducted their personal lives in ways which we would want our youth to renounce. Yet it is natural for aspiring athletes to imitate their athletic heroes. The separation of their athletic abilities from the quality of their personal lives is sometimes too subtle a distinction for an impressionable youth, especially when those personal lives are made to look exciting and glamorous. We shall look at specific instances of this problem in the next chapter when we turn to the problem of drug use among athletes.

A particularly acute example of the problematic nature of athletic hero worship concerns youths who are poverty-stricken. To them, the achievements, including the financial wealth, of outstanding professional athletes can seem so worthy of admiration that the imitation of them may seem "the way out of the ghetto." But because the actual number of athletes who can actually achieve the financial rewards of professional fame is so minuscule, there is great danger that huge number of poor youths, hoping to "make it" in athletics, will spend inordinate time and energy on the playing fields, which they might better have spent getting a good education and preparing for a good job.

More generally, it is sometimes held to be deplorable to hold up as heroes athletes who perform activities with no practical value to society, when there are others—politicians, scientists, business persons—who, engaged in activities genuinely useful to society, ought to be the real objects of admiration.

Others reply that this is not so obvious. In many cultures, and in the not too distant past of our own culture, the cultural hero was more often than not the soldier. But soldiers, so the skeptics proclaim, are trained killers. Better to establish as heroes and objects of imitation athletes, even if their activities are culturally useless, than to hold up as heroes and objects of imitation soldiers, agents of destruction and death. Perhaps the hero worship of athletes is in that sense a sign of a higher culture!

And in any case, who cares if athletes do not perform activities of great practical value, so long as they stand forth as paragons of excellence? Are we so mired in a functionalist and utilitarian mentality that we can no longer see any value in an activity apart from its practical consequences? Perhaps, again, one of the virtues of holding athletes as heroes is that it reminds us that someone, or some activity, can be valuable and admirable independently of considerations of practical utility. If so, then perhaps we need not be so troubled by the phenomenon of the athletic hero.

In this chapter, we have looked at a number of issues that arise out of a reflection on the relation of sport and society. Already present in that relation, as we have seen, are a host of ethical questions regarding the role of athletes in society, and the ethical standards to which they should be held. In the next chapter, we shall focus on some of those ethical issues which are particularly problematic or instructive.

NOTES

1. Huizinga, *op. cit.*

2. Camus, Albert, "The Wager of Our Generation," in *Resistance, Rebellion, and Death*, translated by Justin O'Brien. New York, Vintage Books, 1960, page 242.

3. A more adequate account of this can be found in the first manuscript of Marx's *Economic and Philosophic Manuscripts of 1844*, in the section entitled "Alienated Labor." See for example *Karl Marx: Early Writings*, translated and edited by T.B. Bottomore. New York, McGraw-Hill Company, 1963, page 120 ff.

4. Ibid, pages 13, 26, 31, 127.

5. Brohm, Jean-Marie, *Sport: A Prison of Measured Time*. London, Ink Links Press, 1978, page 26. For other leftist critiques of sport, see Scott, Jack, *The Athletic Revolution*, New York, The Free Press, 1971, and Hoch, Paul, *Rip Off The Big Game: The Exploitation of Sports By the Power Elite*, New York, Doubleday & Co., 1972.

An instructive article is William Morgan's "Play, Utopia, and Dystopia: Prologue to a Ludic Theory of the State," in Morgan and Meier, editors, *Philosophic Inquiry in Sport*, Champaign, Ill., Human Kinetics Publishers, 1988, page 419.

6. Ibid., page 55.

7. A former student of mine, reflecting on his experience as a lineman on the college football team, observed that one of the lessons he had learned was "to be oblivious to the fact that I was inflicting pain on others." The student recognized that he would have to unlearn that characteristic if he wanted to be a good man.

8. Brohm, *op. cit.*, page 52.

9. Lasch, Christopher, "The Degradation of Sport," in *Philosophic Inquiry in Sport*, edited by William Morgan and Klaus V. Meier. Champaign, Illinois, Human Kinetics Publishers, 1988, pages 403–418. The article was originally a chapter in Lasch's *The Culture of Narcissism*. New York, W.W. Morton, 1979.

10. Ibid, page 403.

11. Ibid., page 415.

12. Ibid., page 403.

13. Lasch, *op. cit.*, pages 410–411 (my parentheses and my emphasis).

14. A similar lesson could be learned by reflecting on what goes on in a typical classroom in a college course. There, say in seminar discussion, the measure of a person is thoughtfulness, intelligence, and sensitivity to the issue exhibited. Yet how often are those measures immediately jettisoned as soon as the class is over, in favor of altogether inferior measures!

15. I am reminded of a popular song of a few years ago which proclaimed a dislike for "short people." No one took the song seriously, but one could imagine a society in which, say, short people were systematically discriminated against economically and socially, in which ideological explanations about the "natural inferiority of short people" were widespread, etc. How different is that from the present situation in regard to accounts of racial difference?

16. The contrast with the previous arguments regarding the athletic superiority of black athletes is stunning. Blacks are superior athletically but, it is implied, inferior intellectually. Women are equal intellectually but inferior athletically. In these dialectical games, the winners seem always to be white males.

17. *Sports Illustrated*, May 28, 1973, page 95.

18. Weiss, Paul, *op. cit.*, Chapter 13.

19. Postow, Betsy, "Women and Masculine Sports," *Journal of the Philosophy of Sport*, Vol. VII, 1980, pages 51–58. Also included in Morgan and Meier, *op. cit.*, pages 359–365.

20. Young, Iris Marion, "The Exclusion of Women From Sport," in Morgan and Meier, *op. cit.* pages 335–341. Originally published in *Philosophy in Context*, Vol. 9, 1979, pages 44–53.

21. Ibid, page 336.

22. Ibid, page 337.

23. Hyland, Drew, "Competition, Friendship, and Human Nature," in *Women, Philosophy, and Sport*, edited by Betsy Postow. Metuchen, N.J., The Scarecrow Press, 1983, pages 162–176.

24. I remember reading a few years ago that the average life expectancy of a football player in the NFL is 53 years, although the average life expectancy for American males as a whole is in the seventies.

25. Hyland, Drew A., "Competition, Friendship, and Human Nature," in *Women, Philosophy, and Sport*, edited by Betsy Postow, Metuchen, N.J., The Scarecrow Press, 1983. See especially pages 163–172.

26. Lingus, Alphonso, "Orchids and Muscles," in Meier and Morgan, *op. cit.*, pages 125–136. Lingus takes body-building as his paradigm case of this tendency. He concludes with the chilling speculation that the cybernetic revolution, which is replacing so much of

our former mental activity by computers, might be making our minds too like orchids, increasingly useless, increasingly showy to mask the uselessness.

27. Weiss, Paul, *op. cit.*, Chapter 1.

CHAPTER TWO

ETHICAL ISSUES IN SPORT

Many of the issues raised in the previous chapter on sport and society focused on what we might call areas of crisis, such as racism and sexism. Clearly, many of these crises point directly to questions of ethics and morality. It is the purpose of the present chapter to focus on some of the crucial ethical issues that arise within the context of sport. We do this in part for the insight that may be available in sport on those specific ethical issues. But they can also serve as examples of the kinds of ethical issues present in sport and the way they can be highlighted and reflected upon.

The important French writer Albert Camus, himself an outstanding soccer player in his youth, once asserted that it was from sports that "I learned all I know about ethics."[1] Since Camus was, among other things, active in the French Resistance during World War II, we can speculate that this remark is something of an exaggeration. If so, it is nevertheless an exaggeration that makes a point. Sports, as many of us have experienced, is indeed an arena where one's ethical values are again and again exhibited, tested, and learned. The very structure of most sports includes an intense involvement not just of the body or the intellect but of the whole person. This immersion, coupled with the intensity of the competitive situation where winning matters, and therefore where the temptation—and often the opportunity—is there to cheat, to intentionally injure, to "do anything to win," easily forces to the forefront ethical issues. In so doing it forces us to take our ethical stand knowingly and self-consciously.

Camus does not elaborate on his claim that it was in sports that he learned all that he knew about ethics. He could have meant something so simple as that he learned all the right ethical lessons from sport, those lessons that the partisans of sport regularly claim that sport teaches, such as fair play, teamwork, sportsmanship. But since this was Camus speaking, a writer wonderfully sensitive to the subtle and problematic character of human existence, I speculate that he was probably not referring to the specific ethical teachings available in sport, which he must have known can be deplorable ethical lessons as well as noble ones. Instead, perhaps he had in mind the way in which sport brings to the fore so many of the fundamental ethical questions, in all their subtlety and complexity, and forces us to take a stand. If indeed, "actions speak louder than words," then for many youths it is in sports that we first are confronted with powerful ethical contexts, learn of their import, and exhibit publically our own ethical standpoints. Most of these ethical issues, of course, are not peculiar to sport—we confront them again and again in our lives generally—but they are especially visible therein. To see this, we shall consider three ethical issues as they arise in sport—two very general and one a more specific issue particularly controversial at present: first, the problem of winning; second, the problem of competition and alienation; and finally, the problem of performance-enhancing drugs in sport.

THE OVEREMPHASIS ON WINNING

One does not have to read much sports commentary these days to recognize that the "over-emphasis on winning," which has long been a national concern, remains an immense problem today. Yet we must begin by recognizing that it is not by accident that the vast majority of the sports that have achieved popularity are highly competitive ones, where the game ends with a winner and a loser, where winning counts. The appeal of competitive sports, and so of the emphasis on winning, is obvious in our competitive capitalist society. Perhaps one way to make this clear is by noting the relative failure to achieve great popularity of sports where winning is not an issue. A few years ago, many liberal souls, in an effort to combat what they regarded as the excessive emphasis on winning in our sports and in our society, developed a slew of non-competitive games where there was no issue of winning or losing: the so-called "new games." Many of them, for example, emphasized the spirit of cooperation: see how long everyone involved could keep a large balloonlike ball in the air. Or frisbee, where a group of people just had fun throwing the frisbee back and forth. For better or worse, most of these "new games" died as fast as they were born. In the ironic case of frisbee, it was transformed into a highly competitive sport, "ultimate frisbee," which has achieved national popularity on college campuses. So the "problem of winning" must begin with the recognition of the enormous appeal to us of sports where winning is at stake. We as a people seem to have little disposition to "solve" the problem of winning by abolishing competitive sport. The problem, rather, is to keep winning in proper perspective.

But what, more precisely, is the problem of winning? It is usually characterized as an "overemphasis" on winning. Placed in a context where the game ends with the determination of a winner and loser, and thus where there is a stake in winning, it will always be tempting for a person immersed in the intensity and passion of that competitive situation to push the rules of the game, to cheat, to injure, and generally to "do anything to win." This situation is exacerbated when winning becomes not just an issue of pride in one's ability (issue enough for prideful athletes!) but carries with it a financial import as well. In the most understandable instance, professional sports teams often feel that they must be winners in order to stay in business (although the evidence for this is not conclusive— witness the early days of the New York Mets!). But often at the college level as well, given the enormous spectator appeal of many college sports, there develops in the minds of college coaches and administrators a huge financial stake in having winning teams. Anyone who reads the sports pages or even watches sports news on television is aware of the abuses to which this emphasis on winning can lead. Recruitment violations, the underhanded payment of athletes, the fixing of transcripts in order to keep athletes eligible to play who otherwise would not even be in school, the condoning and sometimes active encouragement of athletes by coaches to take performance-enhancing drugs, all seem directly related to an exaggerated emphasis on winning.

Individual athletes, imbued with the importance of winning and themselves full of competitive spirit, are presented with often difficult ethical choices. One can look at and experience the desire to win in different ways, ways whose subtle differences are nevertheless ethically decisive. Viewed positively, the desire to win can lead one to try to do one's best, to hustle as much as possible, to "give one's all," etc. In doing so and if successful, one realizes that a consequence will be that one's opponent will lose. But that is, as it were, a derivative phenomenon of trying to do one's best. Critics reply, however, that the effort not just to win but to beat someone, especially under the influence of the warlike rhetoric of some coaches, is the real psychology of the competitive athlete. On this view, the attitude of the athlete bent on winning is fundamentally a negative and alienated one toward the team against which he or she is playing.

Our effort to win translates into the desire to beat someone. It is hardly surprising that such a desire generates some of the worst abuses of the emphasis on winning: a willingness to cheat, to hurt others, to treat members of the opposing team not as fellow human beings and athletes but as enemies—as objects to be defeated without respect or regard for their rights as human beings. Is this phenomenon an inherent necessity of the emphasis on winning? Or can that emphasis be controlled in such a way that an enthusiastic effort to win can be exhibited without its devolving into an alienating and sometimes unethical desire to beat someone else, or as our athletic rhetoric so often puts it, to "destroy" them, to "humiliate" them, to "kill" our opponents?

We have noted that neither in our society at large nor in our sporting community do we seem disposed to abolish games which place a stake on winning. The issue therefore seems to be, how can we put winning in a proper perspective? One of the frustrating things about discussions regarding the emphasis on winning in sport is that they often resolve into a false dichotomy of either/or alternatives. On the one hand, hard-nosed realists give us some version of the phrase attributed to the late football coach, Vince Lombardi, that "Winning isn't everything, it's the only thing." I was once told of a sign in the locker room of the Washington Redskins under coach George Allen which purportedly said, "Losing is worse than death; you have to live with losing." At the other extreme, more liberal folk advocate a version of "It's not whether you win or lose but how you play the game," implying, absurdly to any committed athlete, that winning simply doesn't matter. We are presented, then, either with the view that winning is the only thing that matters—the view of many big-time sporting establishments— or that winning doesn't matter at all.

To state the alternatives this baldly is, I hope, to reveal their inadequacy. No committed athlete, whose passion as well as whose energy and time is invested in a sport, will succumb easily to rhetoric that claims that winning doesn't matter. Winning does matter; it is the immediate goal of every competitive game. Any athlete feels exhilaration at winning and disappointment at losing. These reactions are as natural as they are justifiable. On the other hand, it hardly follows from this that winning is the only goal or value of a sport. Putting winning in perspective may mean recognizing it as a legitimate value, but as only one value among others whereby the quality of our athletic involvement is assessed. Putting equitable emphasis on other values in sport, for example, good health, the ethical lessons to be learned such as teamwork and sportsmanship, the friendships we gain, the fun we have, might be a first but decisive step toward overcoming the worst abuses of the overemphasis on winning. Perhaps we should moderate the Lombardian cliche to read, "Winning is something, but not the only thing."

It is worth noting that the concern with the dangers of overemphasizing winning is primarily directed at those sports organizations which still claim to be amateur, from intercollegiate athletics, to high school and club sports, on down to children's sports organizations such as Little League. The charge is less often leveled at professional sports, where it seems more generally agreed that winning is indeed the overriding value. Pat Riley, the coach of the Los Angeles Lakers basketball team, is apparently given to telling his players that if they want to have fun, they should go to the YMCA, clearly implying that having fun at basketball is no concern of his or of his team. Even at the professional level, however, there are presumed limits on winning. One hopes that coaches like Riley do not encourage their athletes to take steroids, though that might help them win. Still, the concern and the charges regarding winning are more often leveled against the supposedly amateur sports.

Part of the problem, then, might be our tendency, and especially the tendency of young athletes, to take professional sports as the model for all sports. Because, by and large, professional athletes are the very best at their sport, it is understandable enough that they would be taken as the paradigms of athletic ability. It is understandable, as well, that the imitation of their behavior might extend beyond technical ability to the attitudes they bring to the game. Perhaps that is what is inappropriate and should be guarded against at the amateur level. But that is easier said than done, in part because the lines between professional and amateur sports are becoming increasingly blurred. Take the case of big-time intercollegiate sports:

when the football team or basketball team generates thousands and even millions of dollars of income; when the coach of the team is by far the highest-paid person at the university; when the players see themselves quite explicitly as preparing themselves for careers in professional sports rather than attending college for an education; when in any case the players' education and even their living expenses are being paid for; the sense in which we speak of the sport as "amateur" rather than professional becomes a fine point indeed.

Still, it is usually agreed that at least at some levels overemphasis on winning is a problem. We need to ask what practical steps might be taken that will permit other values and goals available in sport to moderate the too-exclusive emphasis on winning. Let us begin at the college level, where, I suspect, the crux of the problem finally lies, and let us take up first the status of the coaches, who are so often blamed for being at the heart of the overemphasis on winning.

An oft-made claim made when one wants to praise a coach is to say that he or she is a "teacher." Rarely when this claim is made does it refer primarily to the teaching of the technical skills relevant to the sport in question. More often, it refers to the "lessons in life" that a coach supposedly imparts to players, and therefore, centrally, to the ethical values that the coach gets across by what he or she says and by the way he or she coaches. Coaches are praised for teaching us self-discipline, teamwork, sportsmanship. But unfortunately, as mentioned earlier, they are all too often blamed for teaching us something very different: authoritarianism, cruelty, willingness to cheat in order to win.

About this I offer the following speculation: When we are praising a coach for teaching us desirable values, the coach in question is likely willing to acknowledge his or her role and calling as teacher. But when being blamed for teaching, say, cruelty or cheating, I suspect that coaches would either deny that they taught that or deny that they were teaching at all. "I was just doing my job, trying to win," they might say. This in turn suggests that no matter how often the epithet is promulgated that coaches are teachers, it is too often forgotten in practice. Perhaps, then, we should take whatever steps we can to deepen the cliché into a reality. We need to assure that coaches regularly think of themselves as teachers of ethical values in addition to sport skills, and to insist that they be understood as such and rewarded (or fired!) as such by administrators and colleagues.

Small steps are being taken in this regard here and there. In many so-called "Division III" colleges (schools which make a serious attempt to keep their sports programs consistent with and in the context of their educational goals) members of the coaching staff are accorded status as faculty members. This is a small but important symbolic gesture in that it formally recognizes the coaches as teachers. Even in larger, so-called big-time schools, the graduation rate of athletes is being increasingly regarded as one measure of the program's success. Schools such as Notre Dame, Duke, Penn State, Villanova, and Georgetown are increasingly recognized for their success in seeing to it that their athletes get a legitimate education. But much more could be done.

Coaches cannot be expected to stop putting undue pressure on their players to win until university administrations stop putting undue pressure on the coaches themselves, until winning stops being the sole criterion by which a coach is rewarded or fired. The criteria for promotion, raises, even retention could include not just victories but the coach's ability as a teacher, which would in turn be evaluated in a similar way to the rest of the faculty. Above all, everything possible should be done so that a coach's self-image is that of a teacher. This, I hasten to add, would guarantee nothing; we are only too well aware that academic teachers' self-image as teachers does not guarantee excellent teaching. But it might increase the likelihood that coaches genuinely conducted themselves as teachers.

How could we begin to put this ideal into practice? Consider an analogy with academic faculty members. Academic faculty are evaluated by a number of criteria, typically something like teaching ability, scholarly productivity, and service to the college or university. To be sure, we worry that some institutions seem to follow a "publication isn't everything, it's the only thing" policy. But by and large, universities, especially the good ones, more or less successfully assess their faculty by these several criteria. Why should not the same hold true for our coaches, now become teachers? Assess their ability and success in part on the record of victories—but only in part. Let their won/lost record be the rough counterpart to an academic's publication record. Typically, a faculty member needs some publications, but a modest number can be offset by outstanding teaching. Similarly with the coaches, we would expect good coaches to "be competitive," but even a modest record could be offset if the coach is judged to be a fine teacher, if the athletic experience given to his or her players is a positive one. Winning, then, would be in a practical sense one criterion, but not the only one in a coach/teacher's evaluation.

I do not think a proposal such as this is a pollyanna one, any more than I think it is among academic teachers. Nor do I claim that it would be a panacea to the ethical problems in sport. It would, however, be a significant change from the procedures in many of our big-time sports establishments. If coaches both thought of themselves as teachers and knew that they would be evaluated on the basis not just of their records but of the educational and ethical values they exhibited and inculcated in their players, it would set up part of the context in which the ethical climate in competitive sport could be improved. It is at least an example of the kind of practical step that might be taken to alleviate the overemphasis on winning in college sport. If that overemphasis were moderated in this decisive sphere, we could perhaps hope for a "trickle-down effect" at the high school and youth sport levels.

We could hardly have a problem of the overemphasis on winning if we did not live in a highly competitive society which emphasized the importance and the value of competition, and so of winning. In such a society as our own, as we saw in the last chapter, it is hardly surprising that our sports of choice would tend to be highly competitive. It is hardly surprising, either, that we would occasionally take that competitive spirit too far in our sport as in our society. But this is to say that the problem of winning, in sport and in society, is embedded in a larger problem, the problem of competition itself. To this second issue, clearly related to the problem of winning, we can now turn.

COMPETITION, ALIENATION, AND SPORT

Proponents of competitive sport often praise its competitive dimension for the good effects it can have. Athletic competition, we are told, develops in our youth the competitive spirit, the desire to win, which will be so important to them in their later life. It teaches us that valued goals require hard work, sacrifice, careful preparation. It teaches us as well to compete fairly, within the established rules, to be gracious winners and good losers. To be persuaded by this catalogue of virtues is to be persuaded that athletic competition is a wonderful thing, something to be encouraged in our youth, and so many of us believe.

But as we know well, others hold a very different and more negative view of competition. Would young athletes be taking megadoses of anabolic steroids, thereby putting their health in grave risk, if they had not been imbued with a "competitive spirit" so distorted that it allowed and even encouraged them to put their long-term health in serious jeopardy for the sake of winning a few more games? Would coaches be cheating and offering under-the-table payment to recruited athletes if "the competitive spirit" had not exceeded all reasonable bounds? Would college administrations be looking the other way while educationally deficient athletes were accepted at their institutions and kept eligible by cheating and by taking courses that are almost farcical? Would athletes be engaging in fights, trying to hurt each other, intimidating each other, taking "cheap shots" at each other, if this same competitive spirit were not so overblown? Directly or indirectly, all these phenomena are manifestations of alienation. Is this not proof positive that the Marxists are right—that competition, athletic or otherwise—causes alienation, and therefore that to affirm and praise athletic competition is perversely to affirm and praise alienation? And who wants to do that?

Let us look more carefully at the connection between alienation and competition.[2] On the one hand, I would speculate that virtually everyone who has participated actively in sports has experienced some form of alienation at one time or another. In its mildest manifestations, this might be simply a slight pique that one's opponent, say, has hit you a bit harder than necessary in a basketball game, or has hit a ball at you a bit harder than necessary in a tennis match. Most of us have played in many a sand-lot game which dissolved into futile arguments about whether a baseball hit was fair or foul, whether a tennis ball was in or out, whether a person was fouled or not in basketball. More strongly, most of us have known people who seem only to play their best at their sport when they are alienated, when they are angry at their opponent, want to hurt them, etc. The frenzies of alienation that some football players work themselves into before games are legend—and appalling. At its extreme, we know that many games are ruined when alienation becomes so explicit that the game dissolves into fisticuffs. The evidence is thus overwhelming and undeniable that alienation is very often, all too often, a component of athletic competition.

But so is friendship. Our obsession with professional, intercollegiate, and interscholastic sports can mask the fact that the vast majority of sports events in the world, played at the sand-lot level, are among friends. For many of us, sports have been an occasion where our deepest friendships were made—with teammates and with opponents—and where, on a continuing basis, those friendships are nurtured and deepened. Very few of us are so perverse that we would have continued to play athletic games throughout our lives if we knew that each of those games would necessarily become alienated. No, the vast majority of our games, from the sand-lot to professional level, are significantly free of alienation. The situation, then, is something like this: We know that any athletic game we play might devolve into alienation. But we are willing to take that risk, because we also know that the vast majority of those games are occasions for friendly competition. The empirical news is that both alienation and friendship sometimes, but not always, accompany athletic competition. What are we to make of this?

First of all, the relation between athletic competition and alienation (or for that matter, between competition and friendship) cannot be a straightforwardly causal one. If, as the Marxists claim, competition caused alienation, then we would expect, in Humean language, for there to be much more of a "constant conjunction" between competition and alienation. If alienation occurred in every athletic contest, or in virtually every one, we could plausibly claim a causal connection. But as we have seen, such is not the case. We must thus formulate the connection between competition and friendship in another way.

To do so, let me introduce a distinction between two different kinds of analysis, a descriptive analysis of a given phenomenon, and a teleological analysis thereof. As the name implies, a descriptive analysis attempts simply to describe, as accurately as possible, the way things actually are, or are for the most part, with the phenomenon in question. No "value judgement" is made regarding the phenomenon, whether it is good or bad, which of its modes or manifestations are superior or inferior, etc. Descriptive analysis attempts to "tell it like it is." There can be various types of descriptive explanation, from the causal analyses of science to phenomenological analyses which eschew causal explanation. But they share the insistence that "the way things are" is what is to be analyzed and explained. In that sense, all descriptive analyses claim in some sense or another to be "empirical." The paradigm in our culture of good descriptive analysis is scientific explanation.

Teleological explanation, on the contrary, appeals not just to the way things are, but the way they ought to be, or are at their best. The word derives from the Greek word *telos*, meaning "the end, good, or perfection" of something. The Greek philosopher, Aristotle, insisted that one simply did not have adequate knowledge of a given entity unless that knowledge included its "final cause"—what the thing will become if it is allowed to develop to its highest capacity.[3] He uses as an example our knowledge of the acorn. Suppose that you had comprehensive knowledge of the molecular structure of an acorn, its varieties, and where it comes from. In fact, suppose that you knew everything about an acorn except this: If it is placed in the right environment and with the proper nourishing, it will become an oak tree. To say the least, you would be lacking decisive information about the acorn. But this knowledge is knowledge of its end, goal, or perfection, what it will become if it is allowed to develop to its fullest capacity. This is its *telos*. It is worth emphasizing that, for Aristotle, becoming an oak tree is the telos of an acorn even though a minuscule percentage of acorns become oak trees. On his analysis, then, the "nature" of an acorn is to become an oak tree, even though a descriptive analysis would point out that this happens in a tiny minority of cases. The measure of nature for teleological analyses is not necessarily what happens most of the time, what is typically the case, but what happens when a thing is allowed to develop to its highest, or "natural" capacity, even if that seldom happens.

Both of these forms of analysis are enormously complex, both have important virtues and great difficulties. This simple outline, however, should suffice to shed some light on the connection between alienation and competition, and friendship and competition. To make the point as forcefully as possible, let us grant to the critics of sport a stronger conjunction between athletic competition and alienation than we allowed above. Let us say that not just occasionally but most of the time sporting events are infected with alienation. On a descriptive analysis, that would be sufficient to claim that competition caused alienation, that alienation was a "natural" consequence of competition, and the partisans of sport would then be in trouble. But teleologists could point out that even if most instances of athletic competition were alienated, when sport achieves its highest possibility, when sport "works," it occurs as an occasion not of alienation but friendship. On this analysis, what is "natural" to sport is its *telos*; the *telos* of sport is as an occasion of friendship. Alienation, then, would be analogous to the acorn that gets squashed by an automobile: it is a "defective mode" of athletic competition, not what is natural to it.

If we now restore our sense that, empirically, in most instances, sporting occasions are occasions more of friendship than of alienation, the case for the teleological analysis is even stronger. Alienation is not the natural consequence of sporting competition but what happens when it doesn't work right, when it is a "defective mode." Competition at its best, when it works, is an occasion of friendship. From this it follows that we ought not to consider abolishing sport because some of its defective instances degenerate into alienation. Rather, we should analyze what the surrounding conditions are which keep sport so often from achieving its telos, as well as what those conditions are which encourage sport to be the best that it can be. We have touched on a number of suggestions above. No doubt many more suggestions could plausibly be developed. But for the teleologist, this, and not a descriptive analysis which might point to abolishing sport because it was "inherently alienating," would be the proper framework of analysis.

For the third issue in our consideration of ethical problems in sport, we shall turn to a much more specific problem which would never arise if sport were not embedded in a context in which winning was sometimes overemphasized and in which competition got out of hand. Let us consider a problem which in the view of many is now a national crisis: the widespread use of anabolic steroids and other performance-enhancing drugs by athletes at almost every level, from the professional ranks down through collegiate and even high school sports.

DRUGS IN SPORT

Let us begin by making some important distinctions which will help us understand the particular ethical issues involved with drug use in sports. We should first note that any contemporary discussion of drugs in sport takes place within a social context in which there is national concern—some would say hysteria—regarding the use of so-called "recreational drugs" in the population at large. These drugs include marijuana, cocaine, crack, and heroin. To be sure, there is a considerable problem among athletes concerning the use of drugs such as these. But it could be argued that there is nothing peculiar to athletes about this problem. All the reasons why athletes should or should not avoid these drugs hold as well for the population at large. The controversy within the sporting world centers instead on the use of so-called "performance-enhancing drugs," and without question the heart of the controversy concerns the increasingly widespread use of anabolic steroids by athletes. These drugs are "performance-enhancing" because, it is claimed, significant dosages coupled with strenuous training bring about a quick and marked increase in muscle strength and size.[4]

Until about five years ago, there was nothing illegal about the purchase and use of anabolic steroids. In recent years, however, they have been declared illegal, and now are banned by the International Olympic Committee, the NCAA, the professional sport leagues, and indeed, the vast majority of formal sport organizations in the country. The reasons for their banning are no doubt manifold. Perhaps their association—rightly or wrongly—with "recreational" drug use is a factor. Other reasons have been cited as well: The reports of various health risks involved with the taking of the drug in the large dosages supposedly favored by athletic users, the sense of an unfair advantage for drug users over non-users, the suspicion that there is something "unnatural" about a steroid-aided body build-up (although anabolic steroids are derivatives of testosterone, the "natural" male hormone), all are cited as reasons for banning the use of steroids and other performance-enhancing drugs.

However, because of their apparent success in increasing muscle size and strength, their banning hardly has brought about the cessation of use among athletes. To the contrary, most estimates suggest that the use of steroids has increased enormously since they were banned. There is now widespread evidence of their use by high school and even middle school youth. Not surprisingly, there is a concerted effort to discourage their use. Punishments have been established, well-known athletes who are non-users make public-service announcements condemning them, and in numerous other ways their use is discouraged.

If there was universal agreement about the legitimacy of banning the use of performance-enhancing drugs, there would not be a serious ethical problem. Of course there might be various problems of enforcement, detection, cheating, etc., but these situations in principle would not be ethically problematic. The ethical problem arises because a number of voices have been raised against the legitimacy of banning their use. It has been argued that their banning is an unjust incursion into the right of athletes to do everything they can to enhance their ability. Moreover, these critics have pointed to a host of ambiguities present in the arguments put forward by defenders of prohibition, which give that defense an impression of arbitrariness. To understand this controversy and the ethical issues contained therein, we shall look at the arguments both of the defenders of the ban on performance-enhancing drugs and their critics.

When asked to defend the prohibition of these drugs, supporters of the bans usually point to issues of danger to health, of fairness, coercion, the character of "true" sport, and the athlete as role model.[5] To begin, there is considerable evidence that at least some of these performance-enhancing drugs pose significant health risks to users. This is especially so given the "megadoses" employed by some athletes, who take quantities of the drug far in excess of what would be allowable in any carefully controlled experiment. In particular, there are reports that use of anabolic steroids in large doses can cause liver cancer, shrunken testicles and impotence in men, masculinization in women, loss of hair, and serious acne. There are also apparent psychological effects, the most notable of which is a marked increase in aggressiveness and inclination to violence. Given these dangers, proponents of prohibition argue that these drugs should be banned on health grounds.

Because of these dangers, and because in any case the drugs are prohibited, many athletes will wish not to use them. This leads directly to the second argument, the issue of fairness. Some athletes will be foolish enough (or committed enough!) to overlook the danger to their health if it will help them improve their athletic ability. Those athletes will thereby have a significant advantage over athletes sufficiently concerned about their health not to take steroids. Why, it is asked, should these sensible people have to be at a clear disadvantage compared to people willing to take drugs no matter what the cost to their health? Surely there is manifest unfairness involved here, an unfairness best countered by banning the use of such drugs altogether.

This in turn leads directly to the third argument, concerning coercion. Take an excellent football lineman who has strong career aspirations to play professional football. He learns that a large percentage of National Football League linemen (80% by some estimates) use steroids to "bulk up." This puts the player in a position, it is argued, where he virtually must use steroids himself if he wants to be competitive. He is thus "coerced" into taking steroids, which in principle he might prefer not to take, and this is unjust. Again, the proposed solution to the injustice is to ban the drugs altogether.

A fourth argument claims that the use of performance-enhancing drugs changes the nature of the "persons" playing and so disobeys the ideal of the sports contest.[6] That is, a fair athletic contest is supposed to be among athletes who have "naturally" conditioned themselves to do their best. If Edwin Moses finally loses a hurdles race because he is forced to race against the Bionic Man, no one would call it a fair race. So with steroids, steroid-enhanced athletes are not naturally but artificially developed, and that changes the whole nature of the contest. The Bionic Man, in this argument, is just a more extreme version of the steroid-enhanced athlete. Both are "unnatural," both undercut the true nature of the sports contest, which is supposed to be between persons who test each other's athletic ability—not the respective ability of their bodies to respond successfully to the injection of drugs or other artificial enhancements.

Finally, the point alluded to in Chapter 1, that athletes often function in our society as heroes to our youth, offers another argument for the proponents of prohibition. Youths imitate their heroes. If athletes are—and surely they are—the heroes of many of our youth, then those youths will imitate well-known athletes. If those athletes use steroids, that characteristic, too, will be imitated by our youths, to their potentially serious detriment. There is already considerable evidence that this unfortunate tendency has already set in. As mentioned earlier, many high school and even middle school athletes are now using steroids, presumably in imitation of their college and professional athletic idols. To prevent this "trickle-down effect," the use of performance-enhancing drugs should be banned for all, or so the argument goes.

These arguments—if I have set them out well—seem persuasive enough. They have certainly persuaded the vast majority of people, including virtually all administrators of sports organizations who vote to ban performance-enhancing drugs. But they have failed to persuade some thoughtful critics, who have pointed out that the arguments are often founded on some confusing ambiguities and hide some dangerous threats to human autonomy. Let us turn next to some of the objections raised to the above arguments.[7]

Such critics initiate their objections by raising some definitional ambiguities, beginning with the whole question of what counts as a "drug," or a "foreign" substance. The very notion of a "drug" is, first of all, notoriously difficult to define. But in any case, we regularly use all sorts of substances that are counted as drugs, and it would be hard to imagine their being banned to athletes. Caffeine is a drug, as is aspirin, alcohol, nicotine, and many of the substances we use daily as part of our regular diet. Are we to ban these? Athletes by this standard would be denied some of the most basic medicinal contributions of science and technology that we all use every day. Moreover, some of the banned substances do not seem to be drugs by any definition. Consider "blood doping," a practice whereby one withdraws and stores one's own blood, then later reinjects it, the purported effect being to increase one's ability to process oxygen. One's own blood is hardly a "drug" or "foreign" substance. For that matter, testosterone, the basic ingredient of anabolic steroids, is a "natural" substance, a male hormone. Furthermore, in the case of blood doping, there has been no evidence so far that it has dangerous health effects. Why, then, should it be banned, and why especially should it be banned in the category of "performance-enhancing drugs?" So, critics argue, the proposal to ban drugs hides a web of ambiguities regarding the very notion of a "drug."

The response to this has been to attempt clarification by a number of distinctions. We have already alluded to the distinction between "recreational" and "performance-enhancing" drugs, where the issue particular to sport concerns the latter. A further distinction has been drawn between these and "restorative drugs," drugs that are given not to healthy athletes to enhance performance but to injured or unhealthy athletes to restore the ability to play according to their original levels. Thus aspirin for a headache, or tape for a sprained ankle, would be restorative and not banned, whereas steroids or blood doping would be performance-enhancing and therefore banned.

But this distinction is not so clear-cut as first might seem. Some drugs seem to function both to restore and to enhance. In any case, is my ability to play not "enhanced" if I take aspirin to fight a headache on the day of a game, or take a cortisone injection (itself a steroid!) to ease the pain from Achilles tendonitis? Or take the fascinating case of the kind of operation performed on the great middle-distance runner, Mary Decker Slaney a few years ago. Because of her strenuous training and the massive build-up of her leg muscles, her muscles had "outgrown" the sheaths which contained them, causing her great pain. An operation was performed, slitting the muscle sheaths so that her enlarged muscles would have more room, thereby relieving the pain. On the one hand, the operation seems "restorative," since it relieved pain. On the other hand, the pain was caused by her excessive training which had "unnaturally" built up her muscles; Slaney could have dealt with the problem just as well by slackening off on her training. The clear purpose of the operation was to enhance her performance by allowing her to develop her muscles even further than she had previously been able to do. Was the operation restorative or performance-enhancing?

According to critics, similar kinds of ambiguities and confusions affect the specific arguments against drug use. The first one, recall, concerned the health risks incurred by athletes who use such drugs. W.M. Brown, among others, has pointed out that the evidence regarding danger to health is often sketchy and impressionistic, not carefully studied under controlled conditions and with controlled amounts of the drug. Still, the basic strategy of the critics here has been to grant, for the sake of argument, that there might be dangers to health involved. But, they point out, many of the most popular sports, such as football, are inherently so dangerous to a person's health as to make the health dangers of steroids pale in comparison. Surely the number of football injuries alone vastly exceeds the number of health failures attributable to steroids in all sports. If we are to begin banning activities because of their danger to health, these critics continue, we will surely have to begin by banning many, if not most, of the sports in this country, activities which have long ago proved more dangerous than the use of steroids.

The point of this objection, we can see, is to accuse its proponents of arbitrariness. If we are urged to prohibit such drugs on the principle that activities dangerous to health should be prohibited, then we should either abolish all such activities— including many of our sports themselves—or none. Alternatively, we might settle on some estimated "degree" of health risk. But again, it has by no means been established that the use of steroids is more risky to health than, say, football, boxing, or rock climbing. So it can look as though the appeal to the principle of health as a basis for banning performance-enhancing drugs is arbitrary.[8]

The argument from "fairness" seems to fare no better. This argument, recall, is that performance-enhancers give users an unfair advantage over non-users, who no longer have an "equal chance" to do well. But fairness, as W.M. Brown points out, refers for the most part in sport not to the particular individuals involved but to the rules of the game.[9] A game is "fair" if everyone involved follows the rules. If we extend the notion of fairness to include "equality" or even "equal steps taken to train," things become ludicrous. The very idea of most games, as Brown points out, is to test inequalities. If I practice two hours per day for an event but my opponent practices three, does he have an "unfair advantage" over me? In the name of "equal chance," should he be required to curtail his training? (This is not a frivolous objection. Recall the movie "Chariots of Fire," which portrays how, in a bygone era, any training for an event was considered unsportsmanlike).

Consider, for that matter, the "unfair advantages" that

are everywhere in sport: the unfair advantage of a seven-foot
tall basketball player over his five foot opponent, the unfair
advantage of a boy growing up in Vermont who takes up cross-
country ski racing over his opponent who grew up in Florida,
the unfair advantage of the female equestrian whose wealthy
parents have a stable of horses, over her opponent who grew
up in the ghetto. In short, sport, like life, is full of inequalities,
and if those constitute unfair advantage, sport could hardly get
started at all. In this light, the claim that performance enhancers
offer unfair advantages to users once again can seem an arbitrary appeal to a principle almost never employed in regard to
similar inequities.

As an example of the problems with the first two arguments, consider a phenomenon which I have been told is
occurring presently.[10] In recent years, African-American body-
builders have increasingly been dominating the various body-
building contests around the country. White body-builders,
perhaps making excuses but perhaps correct in their analysis,
have concluded that part of the reason for this dominance is
that dark skin highlights the definition of muscles, so important
in these contests, much better than light skin. To compensate,
they have been literally baking themselves at tanning salons so
that they can make their skin nearly as dark as their black
colleagues.

Suppose that the hypothesis of the white body-builders is
true. On the one hand, if true, there is a manifest advantage
for blacks in the sport of body-building. Every black body-
builder begins every contest with an "unfair" advantage. Are
we therefore to establish two "separate but equal" contests?
Moreover, one can plausibly speculate that the health danger
of contracting skin cancer from these "megadoses" of tanning
is at least as great as the danger of liver cancer from steroids.
Are we therefore going to prohibit excessive tanning (and how
would we define "excessive"?) on the part of white body-
builders? Presumably not. But the parallel to the case of ste-

roids points out how arbitrarily selective we can be in our choices of what is and is not allowed.

The third argument, from coercion, claimed that drug users, by taking the drugs and thereby enhancing their abilities, put coercive pressure on non-users to begin using the drugs on pain of no longer being able to compete at the same level as the users. Here again there is considerable ambiguity over what is and is not "coercion." No athlete is literally forced to use drugs just because others do. He or she always has the option of continuing non-use and accepting a lower level of achievement as a consequence. As W.M. Brown says, "Athletes, as well as the rest of us, must weigh the risks and benefits of the choices they make; no one forces them to seek Olympic gold."[11]

Consider two examples from other walks of life. Imagine an extremely conscientious student who, in an effort to do well, stays up late at night, perhaps with the use of sleep inhibitors, to do extra-credit work; does she "coerce" her fellow students into doing the same? Or consider a young executive, anxious for advancement, who stays at the office, say, until 10:00 at night; I have a family and want to come home at 5:00 in order to spend time with them. Am I "coerced" to ignore my family if I want to advance? In short, it would probably be more accurate to say that non-drug using athletes are put under pressure to use drugs by the example of those who do. But all sorts of pressures abound, in sport as in the rest of life. We give in to some pressures, choose to resist others. Why should the case of performance-enhancing drugs be any different?

When we turn to the fourth argument concerning what constitutes a "natural" person and the ideal of the sports contest, ambiguities once again are present. The claim, recall, is that a steroid user is an "artificially-enhanced" athlete, not the natural person who is supposed to be tested by the contest. But critics reply, what a "natural" person is and is not is by no means clear-cut, especially in this technological age.

In the first place, athletes, especially world-class ones, are already abnormal, if not unnatural, by virtue of their diet, commitment, and especially their training. To make the point, let me cite the example of a student-athlete, a football line-backer, in the early 1970s, who once told our Philosophy of Sport class that he did not lift weights, as some were beginning to do, because it was not "natural." "When I go out on the field, I want it to be the real me, not some artificial monster built up by weights," he said. This remark seems charmingly naive today, in a time when virtually all athletes in every sport use weight training as part of their regimen. Yet it is exactly the kind of remark made by opponents of drug-use! What counts as "natural," that is, is a function in part of social conventions. As earlier observed, the movie, "Chariots of Fire," portrays an earlier time in our own century when any kind of training constituted an unnatural and unsportsmanlike intrusion into the ideal of sport. Nowadays, heavy weight training is considered compatible with our changing ideal of what is "natural," but performance-enhancing drugs are not. Who is to say what the ideal will be like in the next decade? In any case, the inconstancy of our concept of what is a "natural" person and what is the ideal of sport make them difficult and apparently arbitrary standards to which to appeal as a grounds for prohibiting drug use.

Finally, the propensity of youths to imitate the behavior of their athletic heroes is offered as a reason to prohibit drug use among athletes. Again, the danger of arbitrariness is present here. We do not prohibit by law the use of alcohol by athletes, though we know very well that young athletes might imitate that. We do not demand that well-known athletes live celibate life styles, or speak in grammatically correct sentences, or limit their conduct in other ways in order to insure that they are "good models" for our youth. True enough, we hope that happens. We praise those athletes who do and deplore those who don't act as such models. But we do not demand that they do on pain of penalty. Why should we do so in the case of performance-enhancing drugs?

The general critical attack on the arguments forwarded by proponents of prohibition centers on a host of ambiguities that plague those arguments. But the more positive arguments of those in favor of "free choice" regarding performance-enhancing drugs raise important ethical issues regarding paternalism and autonomy. We can turn to those issues now, beginning with a clarification of some of the key terms and concepts in the debate.

Whenever we prohibit certain activities of individuals, even though they might wish to do them, on grounds that it is in those individuals' own interest so to prohibit them, we act paternalistically. Laws requiring the use of seat-belts, or laws requiring motorcyclists to wear helmets, are good examples of paternalistic laws. It is important to realize that what makes such actions paternalistic is that the import of the rule is to protect those being prohibited. The law against murder, for example, is not an instance of paternalism, because it is intended to serve not the murderer but the person threatened with murder. The more one is disposed, or the more a society is disposed, to have laws and norms prohibiting people from actions on the grounds that those people need to be "protected from themselves," the more paternalistic the person or society.

What, then, is the problem with paternalism, since it seems in principle generous and well-intended? The problem is that it constitutes an interference with a person's autonomy or freedom. Those who place significant weight on the value of personal autonomy and freedom are bound to be troubled by instances of what they are likely to label paternalistic interference with one's autonomy. People who are strongly opposed to paternalism, who place particular emphasis on the value of autonomy even when that autonomy risks allowing people to bring harm on themselves, are often called libertarians. One of the great statements of the libertarian, anti-paternalistic standpoint is formulated by the 19th century thinker, John Stuart Mill, in his book *On Liberty*. Mill states,

. . . the sole end for which mankind are warranted individually or collectively in interfering with the liberty of action of any of their number is self protection. That the only purpose for which power can be rightfully exercised over any member of a civilized community, against his will, is to prevent harm to others. His own good, either physical or mental, is not sufficient warrant.[12]

Libertarians, then, count harm to others as the only consideration which legitimizes constraining the autonomy of individuals. Thus laws against murder, robbery, and yelling "fire" in a crowded theatre as a joke, are justified by the threat of harm to others. But seat-belt laws, helmet laws, and other laws which prohibit me from doing this or that "for my own good" are, from the libertarian standpoint, unjust intrusions on my personal autonomy.

Things can get fuzzy when this principle is applied to certain examples, however. Consider the question of laws against suicide. If the only one "hurt" here is the person committing suicide, then on libertarian grounds such a law is unjustified. But is the suicide the only one hurt? What about the family? What of friends, neighbors, perhaps young people who looked up to the suicide as a model?

Still, the libertarian principle is clear enough. Usually, it is amended by a number of provisos, including some reference to the principle of "informed consent" or that the action in question be done by "a consenting adult." The principle of informed consent insists on two provisos, that the individual in question perform the action with adequate knowledge of its consequences, and that the action be done voluntarily. Thus, to take the example of steroids, it would be wrong not to inform potential users of the dangers of steroids, and it would certainly be wrong literally to force anyone to take them. But so long as the individual is informed of the risks, and is not forced to do so, he or she should be free to take or not take performance-enhancing drugs.

The force of the "consenting adults" principle is primarily to make an exception of children. Here libertarians agree that children cannot be considered autonomous, mature individuals capable of weighing the pros and cons of risky activities and choosing intelligently. Therefore a kind of temporary paternalism is allowed regarding children. They can be prohibited against their will from doing things that eventually they will be allowed to do, but the prohibition will only last until they reach adulthood. Thus, again to use the case of steroids, a libertarian might be sufficiently impressed with the dangers of steroids to allow that children should be prohibited from using them. But that prohibition should end when the individual becomes an adult.

The latter principle is sometimes known as "soft paternalism," and has played a significant role in the ethical debates regarding performance-enhancing drugs. Soft paternalism will allow the paternalistic prohibition of risky activities in the case of children, and perhaps mentally impaired individuals, but only temporarily. As soon as the individual demonstrates the capability for mature, autonomous decision making (or more often, as soon as the age of majority is reached), soft paternalism releases its hold on the individual. Indeed, part of the justification by the advocates of soft paternalism is that they exercise that paternalism on children precisely to prepare them safely and prudently for full, and fully autonomous, adulthood. Thus a libertarian who is a soft paternalist, such as W.M. Brown,[13] will advocate the prohibition of steroids and other potentially dangerous drugs for children, but not for adults. This distinction, of course, is often unclear and arbitrarily drawn. Perhaps libertarians would agree that high school athletes should be prohibited from using steroids and that professional athletes should not. But what about college athletes, who are in many ways at the very center of this controversy? If we take the arbitrary determinant of age—say, twenty-one years—some of them are adults, some not. "You may begin taking steroids when you are a senior," sounds rather silly. Still, if the soft paternalistic position is taken, some more or less arbitrary standard will have to be decided upon.

Hard paternalism, on the other hand, entails the belief that paternalistic interference in the autonomy of persons for their own good is justified even in the case of mature, consenting, informed adults. Thus, in a state with a helmet law for motorcyclists, the hard paternalist will be untroubled even if the motorcyclist—say, a thirty-year-old—is fully informed of the dangers of injuries to the head without helmets, but so enjoys the feel of the air on her head that she prefers to take the risk and drive without a helmet. The hard paternalist will still say that it should be prohibited, for the good of the cyclist.

Thus the philosophical basis of the ethical controversy over performance-enhancing drugs in sport centers on the contrasting positions of paternalism and libertarianism. The more strongly committed you are to the principle of autonomy or freedom as the overriding principle of human life, the more opposed you will be to any limitation on that freedom, even when it involves the risk of harm to the actor. Persons with this commitment, such as W.M. Brown, follow out consistently the consequences of that commitment. They argue that information on steroids and any other performance-enhancing drugs should be widely distributed, the drugs themselves should be made generally available, and every adult individual should then make a free and informed decision as to whether or not to use the drugs.

Those, on the contrary, who are committed to other principles of human conduct, such as the conviction that we have a responsibility to protect people from harming themselves, will argue that these principles may at times override the principle of autonomy (to which they may also, to a moderate degree, be committed). They will contend that performance-enhancing drugs should be outlawed for everyone in order to protect athletes from being so carried away in their desire for victory that they will even seriously harm themselves in order to "get an edge." An individual's decision on this controversy will always depend in part on where he or she stands on that spectrum whose two poles are the strong libertarian who believes that autonomy is always the overriding principle of human conduct, and the strong paternalist who believes that autonomy is at best one principle among many, and often not the one of overriding importance.

The libertarian objections to the prohibition against steroids set out above are challenging ones. What sorts of response to those objections can proponents of prohibition make? I want to set out several of the most common and the most challenging responses. The first attempts to turn one of the libertarian criticisms of the prohibitionist argument back on itself. Recall that the libertarian critique often pointed to the ambiguity or opacity of certain of the central concepts in the prohibitionist position. What a drug is, what "fairness" is, what a "person" is, what the ideal of a sport contest is, all were challenged on the grounds that they were so opaque as to be useless in determining what should and should not be allowed. Yet libertarians, at least those like Brown who adopt the "soft paternalist" position that consenting and informed adults should be free to use steroids but children prohibited therefrom, are in danger of appealing to a standard no less arbitrary and ambiguous. After all, when does an individual genuinely become a "consenting and informed adult?" Surely, the prohibitionists can object, no one will be bamboozled by arbitrary age determinations: "All people over age 21 (or 18, or 16, or whatever) are capable of making mature, intelligent and informed judgments; before that age, they are incapable." No one will seriously believe that. Obviously, the determination of when someone really does have the maturity to make such delicate decisions involving conflicts between goals desired and risks to one's health is hardly less opaque than what a person is, or what a drug is. Why does the libertarian, as it were, reject the appeal to some opacities and accept the appeal to others? If appeals to ambiguous distinctions are unacceptable, must not the libertarian swallow hard and say that drugs should be permitted for everyone, even young children?

Regarding the issue of fairness, Brown's claim, that the concept of "fairness" refers to obedience to the rules of the game rather than to who may play, could be countered by pointing out that, in fact, no such distinction is consistently made. In wrestling and boxing matches, weight classifications are established; it is deemed "unfair" for a 200 pound boxer to fight a 150 pounder.[14] Sex segregation is typically practiced in sports which put a premium on physical size, strength, and speed. Age classifications are established in many sports, from tennis to road racing. All of these are limitations on who may play and under what conditions. Thus a prohibition on steroid-enhanced athletes would hardly be the only instance in sport of limitation on who can play and under what conditions.

This rejoinder in fact raises a number of complexities. The examples of weight, sex, and age classification serve not to prohibit individuals from playing at all but to separate them into categories which will presumably allow for fairer, more exciting contests. It is not that 200 pounders are not allowed to box; they are simply not allowed to box lighter boxers. They are confined to boxers of their own weight range in order to assure fairer contests. By this analogy, our attitude towards athletes who use performance-enhancing drugs should be not to prohibit them from competing but to put them in a separate category from non-drug users. I have heard that this is in fact now occurring in some body-building contests, where "open" and "drug-free" categories have been established.

The problem with this is how to establish separate categories which are more or less equal. Boxing and wrestling have been moderately successful at this in regard to weight categories. Though in boxing the heavyweight class tends to be the "glory" class, boxers (and wrestlers) in the lighter weight categories are still accorded significant status. But such is hardly the case with sex-differentiated sports and most age-differentiations, where too often women's sports and the "masters" age categories are consigned to second-class status. The obvious fear, then, would be that if drug-enhanced and drug-free categories were established in sports, and assuming that the drug-enhanced athletes would indeed have size and strength advantages, the drug-free athletes would receive a *de facto* second-class status. This could cause even worse social problems than is presently the case. Still, this case is a fair example of the kinds of complexities that arise when one adopts as one's standard that distinctions should be consistent and non-arbitrary.

A third response to libertarian objections defends and clarifies the claim that if steroids are permitted, many athletes will be "coerced" into using them against their will in order to be able to compete with willing users. The libertarians, recall, objected that "coercion" is hyperbolical in this context. No one is "coerced;" one always has the option of choosing not to use the drugs and competing at a lower level. In Brown's words, "no one forces them to seek Olympic gold."[15] The most one could say is that certain pressures—not coercions—would be placed on athletes to use steroids. But athletes are constantly subjected to all kinds of pressures, some of which they will resist and others to which they will succumb.

It could be replied that this is an excessively abstract claim. No one may be forced to seek Olympic gold, but consider an athlete who has committed, say, ten years of his or her life to that project, passing up other career opportunities in order to practice most of every day to become an Olympic discus medalist. Suppose that athlete then discovers that most of the competition is using steroids and thereby gaining a competitive edge likely to assure victory; the athlete may understandably feel placed in a situation where he or she says, "Either I throw away the work of the last ten years and start from the beginning on a new career, or I take steroids in order to remain competitive." It might be argued that, although abstractly this is an actual choice, psychologically it is tantamount to coercion, or at least to unacceptably strong pressure.

Alternatively, and as the last point suggests, prohibitionists could accept the point that, in the strict sense, literal coercion is not at issue here, but rather certain degrees of pressure. But at what point does pressure become great enough to amount to coercion? More generally, don't we still have to decide, in athletics as in the rest of life, what counts as acceptable pressure and what counts as unacceptable pressure? If a professor presents a student with the alternative of either flunking the course or granting the professor sexual favors, we would hardly accept as a defense the professor's claim that he or she didn't "coerce" the student but gave a choice. So in athletics, we must decide upon what are and are not acceptable levels of pressure. We might decide that the kind of pressures placed on athletes to risk their health by using steroids is unacceptably high, and therefore that drug-use should be prohibited.

The fourth response concerns the phenomenon of hero worship. Athletes do serve as role models for youths, will be imitated by them, and therefore, if the athletes use performance enhancers, it is all too likely that the children will too. Critics object that the athletes didn't ask to become role models, and that it is therefore unfair to demand that they be ethical paradigms. In any case, parents are supposed to be role models too. Every parent does lots of things which he or she does not allow the children to do, so why should things be any different with the athlete? Again, the response to this could be that the argument is excessively abstract, and takes place in a social and psychological vacuum. The fact of the matter is that, particularly in our culture where athletics receive so much media coverage, top-level athletes are extremely charismatic. They will be imitated by young people, and they will especially be imitated by them in actions having to do with the possibility of enhancement of athletic ability. Therefore, whether they asked for it or not, athletes do have a social responsibility to conduct themselves as acceptable role models for youth.[16] One dimension of this responsibility to others includes, so the argument might go, refraining from the use of performance enhancing drugs.

This argument raises a more general issue which is at the heart of the libertarian/paternalist controversy: what is our conception of ourselves as individuals? Let me suggest two different conceptions, which characterize the libertarian and paternalist standpoints respectively. The libertarian position seems founded on a view of the individual which we might call "monadic" or "atomistic." The very emphasis on "autonomy" gives us the clue here. Autonomy comes from the Greek, *autos*, "self" or "oneself." The autonomous individual is one who does things himself, who acts "on her own." This is a conception, then, of the individual as an independent, literally autonomous "monad" or "atom," who may, of course, enter into relations with others, but whose relations with others are not essential to what they are as individuals. By this standard, the chief (in the most extreme cases, the only) responsibility of the individual is to oneself. Examples of the monadic conception of the individual would include the "I" of Descartes' famous "cogito," the Nietzschean "overman," and Emerson and Thoreau's "self-reliant" individual.

The paternalist, on the other hand, holds to a significantly different conception of the individual, which I will call "relational." On this view, to think of myself as an individual in isolation from my social community, and for that matter from my world, is an empty abstraction. What I am as an individual is rather a complex set of relations with others. If I am a father, husband, teacher, and athlete, those names all designate modes of relationality with others. "The essence of man is no abstraction inherent in each separate individual. In its reality it is the ensemble of social relations," says Marx in a classic statement of the relational conception of the individual.[17] So also the philosopher Martin Buber opens his famous work, *I and Thou*, by saying, "There is no I taken by itself, but only the I of the primary word I-thou and the I of the primary word I-it."[18]

What we are, on this view, is inseparable from the nature and quality of our relations with others.

An important consequence of the relational view of the individual is that we can no longer think of the individual as having exclusive or even primary responsibility to oneself. One also has, literally, essential responsibilities to others, responsibilities which are part of what one is as an individual. There can be and has been much debate among "relationalists" about what precisely those responsibilities are and how far they extend. The crucial principle, however, is that we do have fundamental and inescapable responsibilities towards others. Consider, to clarify the distinction, a situation where you have a friend who is about to commit suicide. The monadic individual, of whom the libertarian is an instance, will argue that you have no business interfering with the decision of your friend to commit suicide and certainly no responsibility to do so. In fact, strictly speaking, such interference would be unjustified. The relational individual, on the contrary, might argue that you have a responsibility, as a friend or perhaps just as a fellow human, to prevent that individual from doing irreparable harm to him or her self.

The paternalist, then, will justify the prohibition of acts which harm oneself on grounds that we are relational beings, and that that relationality confers upon us certain responsibilities towards others, among which is the responsibility to prevent individuals from harming themselves. Proponents of the prohibition of performance-enhancing drugs clearly found their position on this conception of the individual. Libertarians, on the other hand, more given to a monadic conception of the individual, will argue not only against such responsibility but against our right to paternalistically interfere with the autonomy of others.

Whether you lean more towards prohibition of performance-enhancing drugs or more toward free choice regarding them will depend in part on what conception of the individual you have. Why is the problem a complex and difficult one? In part, I suggest in closing, because both positions, the monadic and the relational, are plausible and appealing. We want to say that, in some sense however difficult to work out coherently, we are both monadic and relational. But that means that we want to appeal both to the rights of individuals to autonomy and free choice and also to the responsibility of persons towards others. Because those commitments are sometimes in tension, we find ourselves faced with difficult, complex, and delicate ethical choices.

The question concerning the prohibition of anabolic steroids and other performance-enhancing drugs is one of those instances. Here, as elsewhere in life, we are forced to balance principles both of which may be justifiable but may also be in tension. In this case, we must weigh the value of autonomy against the relational sense we have of responsibility to others. If we want to hold to both principles, we must decide what the proper balance is. Would the permitting of performance-enhancing drugs in the name of autonomy fail to give due weight to our relational responsibility to others? Or would the prohibition of drugs in the name of civic responsibility trample on the legitimate claims of individual autonomy? Our decision regarding what the proper balance is will tell us much about our understanding of ourselves and of human nature. This long discussion will have been successful if it sheds some light on just what one truly believes about human beings when one decides one way or the other.

But to raise the question of human nature is to raise at an abstract or general level the question, "Who am I?" That is, questions of human nature inevitably invoke as well the question of self-knowledge. Self-knowledge has long been an important issue in the philosophy of sport, especially since it is regularly appealed to by lovers of sport as one of the great lessons and benefits of sports participation. In our next chapter, therefore, we shall turn to a more detailed look at the question of self-knowledge in sport.

NOTES

1. Camus, *op. cit.*, page 242.

2. For a more detailed setting out of the following, see my "Competition and Friendship," *Journal of the Philosophy of Sport*, Vol. V, 1978, pages 27–37. Also printed in Morgan and Meier, *op. cit.*, pages 231–239.

3. Aristotle, *Metaphysics*, Book I, pages 982b, 983a25 ff.

4. In what follows, we shall concentrate our attention on the controversy over anabolic steroids, which is presently at the forefront of the debate. Although many of the issues will be equally relevant to other performance-enhancing drugs, each must be considered independently. To take one example, if we consider the use of "blood-doping," the apparent lack of health dangers involved may lead us to modify our conclusions regarding its prohibition.

5. The *Journal of the Philosophy of Sport* has published many of the seminal arguments in this debate. See for example the article by W.M. Brown (one of the leading proponents of "legalization") entitled "Ethics, Drugs, and Sport" (Vol. VII, 1980, pages 15–23), and the "Special Symposium on Drugs and Sport," including articles by Brown, Robert Simon, and Warren Fraleigh, in Vol. XI, 1984, pages 6–35. There is also a good discussion of the controversy by Robert Simon (a defender of banning the drugs) in his *Sports and Social Values*, Englewood Cliffs, N.J., Prentice Hall, 1985, especially chapter 4. A third source is Morgan and Meier, *op. cit.*, Part IV, "Sport and Ethics," pages 289–328.

6. Both Simon and Fraleigh appeal to this argument, for example, in the *Journal of the Philosophy of Sport*, Volume IX Symposium.

7. The leading proponent of these objections is W.M. Brown in the articles cited, with occasional help from Robert Simon, who, though finally opposed to performance-enhancing drugs, nevertheless tries to take account of the legitimate objections.

8. The problem is exacerbated by noting that some performance enhancers, such as "blood-doping" (the withdrawal, storing, and rein-

jection of one's own blood to increase oxygen intake), involve no known health risks.

9. Brown, *op. cit.*, pages 17–19. There are exceptions to this claim; sex-segregated sports, weight-categories in wrestling and boxing, and age classifications in various sports all specify who can play.

10. My thanks to Elizabeth Fairbend for this example.

11. Brown, W.M., "Comments on Simon and Fraleigh," in "Special Symposium on Drugs and Sport," *Journal of the Philosophy of Sport*, Vol. XI, 1984, page 35.

12. Mill, J.S. *On Liberty*. Indianapolis, Hackett Publishing Company, 1978, page 9.

13. See for example his "Paternalism, Drugs, and the Nature of Sports," *Journal of the Philosophy of Sport*, Vol. XI, 1984, pages 14–22.

14. As an example of the arbitrariness of these distinctions, one might ask whether the difference between a seven-footer and a five footer in basketball, or a 250 pound player and a 150 pounder in football, is any less unfair than the examples of boxing and wrestling.

15. Brown, W.M. "Comments on Simon and Fraleigh," *Journal of the Philosophy of Sport*, Vol. XI, 1984, page 35.

16. Some top athletes take this responsibility quite seriously. I recently saw an interview with the Chicago Bull's Michael Jordan in which he admitted feeling strong pressure not to make even "normal" social and ethical mistakes because he realized that what he did was an object of national attention and imitation.

17. Marx, Karl, "Theses on Feuerbach" in *The Portable Karl Marx*, edited by Eugene Kamenka. New York, Penguin Books, 1983, page 157.

18. Buber, Martin, *I and Thou*, translated by R.G. Smith. New York, Charles Scribner's Sons, 1958, page 4.

CHAPTER THREE

SPORT AND
SELF-KNOWLEDGE

Many of us who have participated in organized sport can recall a coach's pep talk, usually before an important game, which included some such exhortation as this: "Tonight, you're going to find out who you really are," or "Today, you'll find out what kind of man (or woman) you are." Leaving aside the purely hortatory element in such remarks, there seems to be something true in them. It is often and plausibly claimed that athletics can be an occasion for self-knowledge. In part, this is because of the very structure of sport, and especially of organized sport. Sporting contests, because they usually call both for physical and mental activity, involve the whole person; we are less inclined to "hold ourselves in reserve" in sporting contests. Moreover, the intensity, passion, and pride that can inform these contests often calls forth explicit and public displays of courage, sportsmanship, cowardice, or cheating.

Albeit in a more moderate way, sport thus shares with other intense, passionate, and public activities, such as war, the tendency to bring to explicitness revelations of what kind of people we are, whether courageous, generous, and honest, or otherwise. Moreover, as we saw in the last chapter, the competitive structure of most sports brings particularly to the fore our public stand on a number of ethical issues, from a willingness to cheat to trying to hurt others. It thus does seem to be the case that sport can, thanks to its very nature and structure, bring to explicitness personal qualities that might not always be visible even to ourselves, and thus be an occasion for self-knowledge. In this chapter, we shall want to examine some of the ways in which types of self-knowledge have been claimed in behalf of sport, and what kind of self-knowledge each reveals.

THE SELF-KNOWLEDGE OF PSYCHOANALYSIS

We can begin with what, in our culture at least, is probably the most common sense of "self-knowledge" current, which we might call loosely the psychoanalytic sense of self-knowledge. We can learn much about ourselves by examining both the specific sports that we choose to play, and our mode of involvement in those sports. At least one well-known psychoanalyst, Arnold Beisser, has made something of a specialty of the treatment of psychologically troubled athletes. His book, *The Madness in Sport*, presents a number of case studies, what he claims those cases reveal, and draws from them a number of conclusions about the psychology of American sport in general.[1]

Beisser plausibly suggests that much can be learned about his patients' pathologies by paying attention to the kinds of sport choices they make, and their mode of involvement in their sports. In a case study entitled "The Boy Who Played the Game Too Well," for example, he shows how that player's virtual obsession with "passing off" and being a good "team player" reaches pathological proportions. For Beisser, it proves revelatory of the deep fear of autonomy and being "on one's own" that troubles the player in every facet of his life.[2] In another case, a patient's choice of golf as his sporting pastime reveals both his desire to be in competitive situations where he can be on his own, not dependent on others, and have the opportunity to "beat" others, yet avoid the possibility of physical confrontation and violence which his early background taught him to fear.[3]

Beisser's analyses, as is often the case with psychological

case studies, are suggestive, plausible, and at times provocative. They are, of course, limited to analyses of people whose psychological difficulties have become pathological. But if sport choices and modes of involvement in sport can be informative for people with identifiable psychological pathologies, why should they not, in principle, be equally informative for all people? Proceeding on that hypothesis, we shall look not so much at the specific case studies which Beisser sets out but at the categories of analysis that he employs, categories which may be applicable to anyone's involvement in sport. Those categories seem divided into two general classes which we shall take up in order: the significance of the type of sport one chooses, and the significance of one's mode of involvement in the sport of one's choice.

Consider first what we might call the social status of one's sport choices. Suppose you come from a poor family that constantly had to struggle financially, and your favorite sports are polo, golf, and squash racquets. What does this suggest? Is it an indication of a troubled effort on your part to deny your impoverished background, or does it represent a healthy ability to transcend the social limits of that background? Conversely, suppose you come from a wealthy family and you make the same sport choices. Does that suggest that you are so strongly tied to your social class and its limitations that you cannot break free of them? Or is it rather a healthy sign that you have "come to terms" with your class status and what it signifies? Alternatively, suppose you are an African-American from an impoverished background whose favorite sports are boxing, basketball, and double dutch? Suppose you are a wealthy member of the social register with those same choices? Finally, suppose your choices of sport represent a range of social status: you most enjoy, say, double dutch, basketball, and golf. Does this reveal a confusion on your part as to your proper social class, or a healthy refusal to be limited by social connotations?

Notice in each case that the particular sport choices that you make do not automatically give you the answers to these questions. They must be answered individually by each person involved. Rather, reflection on the social status of one's sport choices enables one to ask the question of the meaning and significance of one's choices in this regard. We have here, then, not a psychological "calculus" for discovering the answer to the question, "Who am I?" but rather a framework for asking those questions which might lead to self-knowledge. We shall discover that the same is true of the other categories of analysis.

Consider as a second category the choice of team sports as opposed to individual sports. Suppose your favorite sports are all team sports, such as soccer, basketball, and lacrosse. Does this reveal a healthy sense of "relationality" on your part, an easy willingness to cooperate with others, even to place your destiny in part in the hands of others? Or does it rather represent, as in the case mentioned above of "The Boy Who Played the Game Too Well," a pathological dependency on others, a fear of being on one's own, of having to take full responsibility for oneself and one's destiny? Again, suppose your sport choices run distinctly to individual sports: you play tennis (you much prefer singles to doubles), golf, and you run an occasional ten-kilometer road race. This could indicate a strong sense of independence on your part, a willingness to take your destiny in your own hands. But it could rather indicate an overly "monadic" personality, an unwillingness or inability to trust others, to cooperate with them in an enterprise such that success or failure must be shared among many. Suppose, finally, that you enjoy both individual and team sports: a nice personality balance or a vacillating confusion? Again we should note that the category supplies not answers but questions, questions which, individually and honestly answered, may lead to self-knowledge.

A third category refers to competitive vs. non-competitive sports. Suppose you enjoy jogging, cross-country skiing, and swimming, but would never think of entering into a race. Does this suggest a healthy self-confidence which does not constantly have to "prove itself" or "beat someone," or rather a fear of

challenging oneself, of losing, of "putting oneself on the line?"
Or do you get utterly bored when someone asks you to throw
a frisbee around, go for a jog, or go fishing, unless that activity
can be turned into a race or contest? Again, your willingness
or unwillingness to enter in competitive situations can tell you
something about yourself. Does your enjoyment of competitive
situations suggest a desire to dominate others, or a perverse
attraction to alienating situations? Does your reluctance to
compete indicate a pathological fear of losing, or of situations
where alienation might arise?

(4)   Consider next the difference between so-called contact and
noncontact sports. A preference for contact sports could suggest a healthy exuberance regarding one's own body and those
of others, a playful enjoyment of physical contact. Or it could
reveal a precariously controlled desire to physically dominate
or even hurt others. A reluctance to participate in contact sports
could manifest a fear of physical intimacy or the desirable absence of a need to physically dominate others. I once had the
occasion to witness a boy who had been suffering schizophrenic
episodes, who somehow managed to play an entire basketball
game without physically touching any of the other players—a
truly remarkable, almost bizarre event.

The issue of contact vs. noncontact sports enables us to
raise a related issue. In our culture, dominated as it still is by
northern European restraint, everyday physical contact, especially among males, is kept within strict conventions (shaking
hands, etc.). Overt public displays of affection are frowned
upon. The conventions of the sporting situation, however, present an interesting and thought-provoking contrast to this restraint. For the athletic context offers to males one of the few
places where they can freely and publically express physical
affection, or for that matter freely express their emotions, without fear of censure. We see in sports male athletes hugging,
kissing, patting each other's buttocks, crying together, all of
which in other social contexts would be viewed with puzzlement
if not alarm. We might well ask, which is the more "natural"

situation, and which set of customs should be more widely disseminated?

Perhaps related to the last category, one's attraction or resistance to participation in coeducational sports can offer considerable insight into one's sexual attitudes. Here the situation is often significantly different for males and females. Beisser recounts a case of an excellent female tennis player which, in less extreme versions, has been experienced by many an accomplished female athlete. "Susan," in Beisser's study, is reluctant to play tennis with her boyfriend because it would place her in an uncomfortable double bind. On the one hand, she could intentionally play poorly and lose to her boyfriend, thereby preserving his presumably fragile masculine ego, but, in her heart of hearts, losing respect for him. Or she could play to her ability, probably beat him, but thereby endanger both his masculine identity and, in his eyes and hers, call into question her own femininity: "But he won't think I'm much of a woman. Maybe he'll think I'm a dyke."[4]

For many men, conversely, the prospect of playing against women athletes, particularly accomplished ones, can be discomforting. What seems particularly troubling here is the possibility of losing. Many men, when confronted with this situation, avoid the genuine confrontation by overtly "fooling around," and making it very clear that they are not "really trying," thereby shielding themselves from the presumed consequences to their ego of losing to a woman.

How can we explain this reluctance, on the part of well-intentioned women to beat men at sports and on the part of men even to confront the possibility of losing to women? Why should beating a man at a game be more problematic than beating a woman, or losing to a woman be worse than losing to a man? It seems clear that somehow, winning and losing at sports in these contexts have been invested with significance regarding one's sexual identity and prowess. It is one thing to recognize the objective absurdity of this association (presumably one's adequacy as a sexual partner is only contingently related to, say, one's tennis ability), but the question persists as to why the association is so prevalent.

One possibility might be that winning or losing is taken as a symbol of sexual dominance. In a culture where, to a much too large extent, male sexuality is still associated with dominance and female sexuality with submission, it becomes more understandable that winning and losing in sport would begin to take on a powerful if objectively absurd sexual significance. This is hardly to affirm that association; to the contrary. Perhaps a recognition of the absurdity of the association of winning and losing at sport with sexual identity can lead us to a reflection on the absurdity of associating dominance with male sexuality and submission with female sexuality altogether.

There are other categories having to do with choices of sport which might be mentioned, and I do not intend this list to be exhaustive. One might, for example, wonder about the significance of spectator as compared to non-spectator sports, or of sports (or positions within sports) emphasizing brute strength or size in contrast to those emphasizing skill or intelligence. All such categories enable us in principle to ask those questions about the meaning and significance of our choices which might be the occasion for self-knowledge.

The second type of issue which might be psychologically informative refers not to the particular sport chosen but to one's mode of involvement in that sport. Beisser's example cited above of the basketball player who refused to shoot but obsessively concentrated on "passing off," or the player in my own experience who avoided physical contact with the other players, are good examples of this sort of category. Let me now point to some other examples, again with no claim to be exhaustive. Indeed, a careful reflection on one's own involvement in sport might lead us to discover what are the salient categories which lead to self-knowledge in each individual case.

Most of us have known people who are "poor losers," who seem not to be able to disassociate losing a particular game from the issue of their own personal worth, who thus overreact to a loss. Conversely, there are people who seem incapable of winning graciously, who insist on gloating over victories and trying to humiliate those whom they have just defeated in the game. These are surely revelatory of character traits. The same is true in the well-known case of the "clutch player," who always plays her best in crucial games or at crucial moments in the game, or conversely, the player who "folds in the clutch," who may be an excellent player generally but who never seems to "come through" in critical moments or in critical games. Consider also the difference between those players who only seem to do their best when alienated from the opposing player or team, when they "get mad," as opposed to players who, on those occasions when alienation occurs, "choke," and are unable to play at their usual level of excellence. Both instances can tell us much about ourselves.

Many other instances could be named in this regard. The phenomenon of the "injury prone" athlete has received significant attention from athletic trainers in the last few years. There are statistically abnormal tendencies for certain players to be injured, and for others, when they do get injured, to recover with astonishing speed. Is there a psychological component to these tendencies? One might consider also the case of the "selfish" player, who plays a team sport as if he were the only player on the field, or the player who plays a sport for which she is ill-equipped physically, say a very small person who chooses basketball, or a tall, gawky person who enters gymnastic competition. All categories such as these enable us again to ask the kinds of questions about our involvement in sport which can lead us to learn something significant about ourselves.

ZEN AND SELF-KNOWLEDGE

But this "psychoanalytic" mode of self-knowledge is neither the only mode of self-knowledge nor the only one claimed in behalf of sport. In recent years, there has been a wave of interest among the sporting community in a phenomenon known as "peak experiences" (a term borrowed from the psychologist Irving Mazlow). That in turn has sparked widespread interest in the possible relevance of Asian thought to the sporting experience. The latter interest has certainly focused on the religion of Zen Buddhism, particularly as it has been popularized for the sporting community by Eugen Herrigel in his seminal work, *Zen in the Art of Archery*.[5] A look at the "Sports" section of most bookstores will usually reveal half a dozen or so books on this sport or that entitled *Zen Tennis, Zen Soccer, Zen Running*, etc., all of which have their source in Herrigel's original foray into this domain. We will want to look briefly at the phenomenon of the "peak experience," then move on to a consideration of the similarities and differences between it and the Zen standpoint with regard to sport, concentrating our attention on the insights of Herrigel.

The term "peak experience," coined by Mazlow, refers to a powerful psychological state occasionally attained, one of particular intensity, meaning, and achievement. One becomes so totally focused on a given activity or experience that everything else pales into insignificance, and dimensions of the activity which usually might be difficult or accomplished only with great effort now seem to occur effortlessly and smoothly. The experience might be one of love or friendship or a difficult cooperative activity. The term quickly caught on in the sporting realm—and with good reason.

Many accomplished athletes have had a similar experience in their sport. Typically, an activity usually regarded as difficult, say, throwing a long pass in football, hitting the tennis ball to the precise desired spot, or shooting the basketball accurately, suddenly seems easy and effortless. Obstacles to one's success, other players or inert objects, are overcome smoothly and with hardly a thought. Time sometimes seems to slow down, as if the activity were being accomplished in slow motion. A sense of utter confidence pervades the athlete's consciousness: he or she "knows" that the ball will be hit properly, or the shot will be made. Kenneth Ravizza, one of the leading researchers into this phenomenon in sport, quotes a number of athletes interviewed about their peak experiences, who offer comments such as this by a football player: "Everything is right, everything is in line, everything is clicking, nothing is opposing me."[6] The great soccer player, Pele, offers the following powerful account of one such experience:

It was a type of euphoria; I felt I could run all day without tiring, that I could dribble through any of their team or all of them, that I could almost pass through them physically. I felt I could not be hurt. It was a very strange feeling and one I had not felt before.[7]

Other qualities are noteworthy about the peak experience. First of all, it does not come to novices. The peak experience is the culmination, typically, of long hours and even years of practice and achievement. If one goes skiing for the first time, or goes on one's first five-mile run, one will be most unlikely to have a peak experience. Indeed, one characteristic of the experience, which gives it the sense of effortlessness, is that the specific activities performed are accomplished "without thinking." Most accomplished athletes have experienced the transition in their ability from the stage where the action performed, say the swing of the tennis racquet or the shooting of the basketball, is a step by step, explicitly cognitive activity ("Make sure my grip is right. Keep my elbow in. Keep my eye on the ball, etc.") to a point where the action "just happens without thinking about it." Indeed, many a coach, after watching a novice player struggle to master a certain skill, will finally exhort, "Stop thinking about it. Just do it!"

This experience, available to accomplished athletes, contains within it a number of issues regarding human cognition and knowledge which contemporary epistemologists would do well to study. What is going on in this transition from explicit, step by step cognitive activity to the effortless, almost intuitive performance of the activity by the skillful athlete? Is it really the case that the action is done "without thinking?" Or has the cognitive activity somehow been transformed from the explicit, conscious level to a more unconscious, almost instinctual level—from our minds to our muscles and bones, as it were?

Perhaps it is simply a different mode of cognitive activity. Athletes, in describing this experience, typically characterize it as involving a very high level of awareness and responsiveness, even though not of the "first I do this, then I do that" variety. One feels especially open, aware, and capable of responding to whatever happens. So it is not literally an experience of being "unconscious" (though we may describe it as such for lack of a better word) but, if anything, a heightened level of consciousness of a qualitatively different sort. But of what sort?[8]

As the above effort suggests, it is much easier to refer to the peak experience than to analyze it accurately and in detail. Nevertheless, most athletes, when the experience is invoked, find resonances in their own experience. Peak experiences are exhilarating moments in an athlete's life. Yet, interestingly, they are not "controllable," in the sense that one can bring them on at will. To be sure, we can prepare to be "open" to such possibilities, both by long hours of practice and by psychological readiness. But they are not literally an issue of "will power." Hence there seems always to be some element of mystery associated with the experience, and this is part of what invites the association with the Zen experience.

I often teach a course entitled "Philosophy of Sport," usually to a class of fifty or so, most of whom are intercollegiate athletes. After having introduced the notion of a peak experience more or less as above, I ask the class how many of them would say that they have had such a peak experience. Usually, virtually all of them affirm that they have. I then ask how many have had a "mystical experience." At most, one or two will raise their hands. There is an aura, especially in the west, surrounding the notion of a "mystical experience" which gives it the sense of being "far out," "weird," and in any case inaccessible to all but a few special initiates. Clearly, my students share an intuition that the peak experience, which they all have had, is very different from a mystical experience, which, they suppose, almost none of them have had. But what is that difference? Let us turn to Herrigel's account of the Zen experience in *Zen In the Art of Archery* to examine this question.

Surely, part of the reason for the aura of inaccessibility surrounding Zen involves the rhetoric of that movement, at least as it is translated into English. In Herrigel's work, for example, we are told of the need to become "unconscious," to achieve "self-forgetfulness," "self-annihilation," that when we become Zen adepts we will have achieved an "artless art," and that in the experience of Zen we shall join with the "unnameable Groundlessness and Qualitylessness—nay more, (become) one with it."[9] These are hardly terms which invite easy understanding. Do these opaque terms accurately reflect the genuinely extraordinary, almost unique "mystical" experience? Or do they misleadingly make inaccessible an experience similar in many ways to the peak experience which so many athletes have had? I suggest that there is much to be said for the latter contention.

Eugen Herrigel studied Zen Archery for six years under the Zen Master, Kenzo Awa.[10] He offers an account of that experience primarily directed to a "western" audience. In the introduction by the well-known Zen instructor, D.T. Suzuki, we are immediately informed of the importance of becoming "unconscious," of getting to the point where our thought no longer "interferes" with the depths of our unconscious. "As soon as we reflect, deliberate, and conceptualize, the original unconsciousness is lost and a thought interferes."[11] This state of "childlike" unconsciousness, we are told, is achieved, or restored, after "long years of training in the art of self-forgetfulness."[12]

As I mentioned earlier, this vocabulary of "unconsciousness" and "self-forgetfulness" seems to adumbrate an experience which is extraordinary, even bizarre. Or does it rather refer to something like the athletic experience described above, when, indeed after "long years of training," the athlete develops from the stage where she has to "think" about each aspect of the desired skill, step by step as it were, to the point where the action "just comes" without that explicit analytic cognitive activity? It is worth noting, in fact, that often when an athlete is having one of these "peak experience" occasions, we speak of him or her as being "unconscious," though we hardly are referring to a "far out" mystical experience. Perhaps, that is, the word "unconscious" is an unfortunate one (especially in a culture dominated by Freudian associations with the same term) which refers not to an esoteric phenomenon but to an accessible experience of a different mode of cognition from the more standard, "analytic" mode.

The term "self-forgetfulness," also introduced by Suzuki in the passage quoted above, plays a significant role in Herrigel's account. The "self" on this view is something fundamentally negative, something to be left behind. Decisive for the Zen adept, we are told, is that,

. . . his experiences, his conquests and spiritual transformations, so long as they still remain "his," must be conquered and transformed again and again until everything "his" is annihilated . . . . . . only the contemplative, who is completely empty and rid of the self is ready to "become one" with the "transcendent Deity".[13]

This will be achieved, we are told, only

By letting go of yourself, leaving yourself and everything yours behind you so decisively that nothing more is left of you but a purposeless tension.[14]

What is this "self" that is such an obstacle, that needs to be overcome if one is to achieve the kind of transcendence promised for the Zen adept? It is possible, to use terminology introduced in the previous chapter, that the "self" in question here is something like the "monadic" self, or as we sometimes express it psychologically, the "ego." Alternatively, the self that must be transcended might be the "epistemological self," that is, the self which explicitly and consciously analyzes and plans, in a step by step manner. If so, the "transcendence" of the self might in fact be nothing more mystical than not letting one's "ego" hinder one's play, or the transformation that occurs in any accomplished athlete in the achievement of that state of mind where the performance of the action "just happens," and no longer requires explicit cognitive activity.

In any case, a crucial result of this achieving of the unconscious and forgetting of the self, as Herrigel emphasizes, is the achievement of what he calls "artless art":

Then comes the supreme and ultimate miracle: art becomes "artless," shooting becomes not shooting, a shooting without bow and arrow; the teacher becomes a pupil again, the Master a beginner, the end a beginning, and the beginning perfection.[15]

This sounds like strange and heady stuff, the sort of experience that surely is inaccessible to most of us. On the other hand, as it is described in Herrigel's actual achievement of the state, it seems considerably less otherworldly:

Bow, arrow, goal and ego, all melt into one another, so that I can no longer separate them. And even the need to separate has gone. For as soon as I take the bow and arrow, everything becomes so clear and straightforward and so ridiculously simple. . . .[16]

So described, again, the experience seems less a mystical (or mystified) one than the sort of ease and smoothness described by skilled athletes in peak experiences.

I have been suggesting so far that there are striking similarities between certain important aspects of the Zen experience (the unconscious, self-forgetfulness, artless art) and dimensions of the peak experience. Such experiences and such similarities can indeed be revelatory of self-knowledge, particularly of the different "levels" of consciousness occasionally available to us. This is not to insist, however, that there are no interesting or important differences between Zen and the athletic peak experience. Perhaps the most striking difference has to do with the more specific goal of the athlete. For the athlete, one main point of achieving this "unconscious" state where the activity becomes an "artless art" is to do well at the sport. It can be speculated that if such peak experiences did not include among their qualities that one played at a superior level, athletes would not be very interested in the experience. Zen Masters, on the other hand, insist that, in the case of archery for example, hitting the target is not the important thing. What counts is the achievement of this higher state of unconsciousness.[17] Even granting this central difference, however (which might itself be a reflection of the excessive "goal orientedness" of western society), the similarities between Zen and the peak experience are noteworthy and thought-provoking.

SOCRATIC SELF-KNOWLEDGE

We would not want to leave a discussion of the psychological aspects of sport, and particularly the issue of self-knowledge, without considering another sense of self-knowledge available to us in sport, one that has a long and honorable tradition in our culture: self-knowledge in the Socratic sense as "knowing what I know and what I do not know," or somewhat more broadly, self-knowledge as knowing one's capabilities and one's limits. A common coach's exhortation, especially to a player given to attempting things beyond his or her capabilities, is to say something like, "Just play within yourself!" The implication here is that part of being an athlete, and presumably, part of what one learns as an athlete, is to know with some comprehensiveness which sorts of moves one is skilled enough to try, which are beyond one's capabilities, and then, to play within those limits.

This last phrase has two aspects: play within one's limits in the sense of not trying to go beyond them, but also play in such a way as to "take it to the limit" each time, that is, to do all that one is capable of. And indeed, good players often accomplish this sense of self-knowledge remarkably well. Players who rarely make mistakes, yet who nevertheless have a significant impact on the game, exhibit this virtue. To know what one can and cannot do and to do all that one can do would seem to qualify as the athletic version of Socratic self-knowledge. It is a remarkable enough achievement within the athletic realm itself. To the extent that it can be made a self-conscious characteristic and perhaps expanded from the confines of one's chosen sport to one's life more broadly, it can serve as a model for a life characterized by the same sort of self-knowledge.

What sort of "self" is it that the athlete knows in this sense? One does not have to develop an elaborate interpretation of Platonic dialogues but can look straightforwardly to the athletic experience to get the answer. In taking one's ability to its limits again and again, one expands those very limits; one "improves." But improvement of one's athletic ability by taking it again and again to its limits is the athletic equivalent of self-development. The self that one might know in this way, then, is not a permanent, finalized or totalized self. It is one that is, or at least should be, always developing. It is a self in movement, a self in transition.

The athlete, we might say, creates the (athletic) self that he or she is, and is in large measure responsible for that creation. There is thus a clear model within the athletic realm for the conception of "self-creation" that has been so important in existential philosophy. It is also present in those psychological standpoints, such as "self-realization" psychology, which have built on that philosophical conception of the self. At least athletically, within this sphere where mind and body interact so intimately, the self, like the athletically skilled body, is one that becomes. But this leads us to the subject of the next chapter, the connection of mind and body as it is exhibited in sport. How are we best to understand this complex interconnection?

NOTES

1. Beisser, Arnold, *The Madness in Sport*. Bowie, Md., Charles Press Publishers, 1977.

2. Ibid, Chapter 3, "The Boy Who Played the Game Too Well."

3. Ibid, Chapter 9, "A Case of Strength Through Sports."

4. Ibid, Chapter 6, "On Being a Woman and An Athlete." See especially page 77.

5. Herrigel, Eugen, *Zen in the Art of Archery*. New York, Vintage Books, 1971.

6. Ravizza, Kenneth, "A Subjective Study of the Athlete's Greatest Moment in Sport," paper presented at Mouvement, Actes du 7ᵉ symposium en apprentissage psycho-moteur et psychologie du sport, Octobre, 1975, Quebec, Canada, page 402.

7. Quoted in Shainberg, Lawrence, "Finding the 'Zone'," *New York Times Sunday Magazine*, April 9, 1989, page 35.

8. Recently, efforts have been made to account for the physiological basis of such experiences. For a good lay account of this research, see the *New York Times Magazine* article, Shainberg, *op. cit.*, page 34 ff.

9. Herrigel, *op. cit.*, page 22.

10. Even his account (*op. cit.*, pages 27 ff.) of the time spent can be rhetorically misleading. "He studied archery almost every day for six years! Wow!," one is invited to wonder. Then I ask my students whether any of them have practiced their sport of choice for less than six years. The account then loses some of its mystification.

11. Ibid, page 11.

12. Ibid.

13. Ibid, pages 26, 30.

14. Ibid, page 52.

15. Ibid, page 20.

16. Ibid, page 88.

17. A westerner might observe that it can hardly be accidental that all Zen Master archers happen to be excellent shooters. One wonders how many students a Zen Master would have if he were a terrible shooter.

CHAPTER FOUR

MIND AND BODY IN SPORT

How many times have we heard it said that "High-jumping (or shooting a basketball, or hitting a baseball, etc.) is 90 percent mental"? Now it would hardly be surprising if someone said "Philosophy is 90 percent mental." What is stunning about attributing this high importance to mental activity in sport is that, at least on the surface, sport seems so consummately a physical activity. After all, many a student goes down to the gym for an athletic workout after a hard day of studying precisely in order to escape primarily mental activity. Can it be that such students are in truth simply going from one predominantly mental activity to another?

No doubt the claim that this or that sport is mostly a mental activity is an exaggeration, but it is probably an exaggeration of a truth. Sport is not a mindless physical activity. Virtually any sport has a very significant mental as well as physical component. It might be the psychological aspect of getting oneself mentally prepared to do one's best, or the development of a strategy for a race or game; perhaps it is one of the myriad "snap decisions" that most games force us to make constantly, decisions which turn the game into the game that it is, turn each of us into winners or losers. If anything, this mental component is becoming more explicit as our various sports develop. An athlete from the 1950s, for example, would be startled to see football coaches sending in plays for the quarterback, or to learn that many college athletes spend almost as much time watching films of themselves and other players as they do on the practice field. How puzzled he or she would be to watch a "point guard" in basketball dribbling slowly up the court, looking over to the coach for the play he wants to execute, then holding up his own hand to signal the play to the rest of the team. So important has the psychological aspect of various sports become that many professional and even college teams have hired "sports psychologists" (a now burgeoning field), to better motivate the players to play to their full potential.

All this emphasis on the mental aspect of sport is as interesting as it is because, notwithstanding the occasional exhortations to the contrary, sport is also a fundamentally physical activity. But that is to say that, more than many of our daily pastimes, sport is a vivid and explicit combination of mental and physical activity. It thus offers a fascinating occasion for reflection on their interaction.

To engage in reflection on the connection of mind and body, however, is to engage in one of the oldest but still most lively issues in philosophy. From the Pythagorean belief in the transmigration of souls, to Christian disquisitions on the immortality of the soul, to Descartes' influential 17th century account of the separability of mind and body, to the latest books by physicalists and phenomenologists, the question of the relation of mind and body, or perhaps more cautiously, of mental and physical activity, has been a crucial issue in the history of philosophy. In what follows, we shall set out only to outline some of the major positions taken in the controversy. We shall then turn to the realm of sport to see which views are confirmed and which disconfirmed by the evidence of sporting activity.

DUALISM

Two of the oldest views on this question were set out as early as Pre-Socratic philosophy: the "dualism" present in the Pythagorean doctrine of the transmigration of souls, and the "materialism" presented in such philosophical positions as

Democritus' "atomism." The Pythagoreans held to a religious conviction that souls, at death, simply transmigrated from the now dead body they had formally occupied into a different body (sometimes not even of the same species). In order to hold this, they had to make a clear distinction between two substances, the body and the soul. Although for Pythagoreans, any given individual was the combination of a certain body and a certain soul, there were two crucial convictions that this view maintained. First, the body and the soul are separable. Indeed, death gets defined by the Pythagoreans as the separation of the soul from the body (so that the soul, now "free" of the body, can migrate into another). Second, given this separability, the "real" person is not the body but the soul; the soul is the crucial dimension in the "personality" of the person.

Plato entertains and passes along this dualist position in his dialogue, *The Phaedo*, which presents Socrates, on the day of his death, persuading those present (most of whom are themselves Pythagoreans) that he is not really going to die, that death is really the separation of soul from body and the freeing of the soul from the body so that it can ascend to the "higher" world of the forms.[1]

When Christianity develops, it seizes upon this dualist view as the philosophical basis for its emphasis on the afterlife. Since the evidence that the body does not live on after death is overwhelming, a belief in the afterlife can be sustained only by arguing that there is something else about the person, the soul, which is separable from the body, does not necessarily die with the body, and therefore can live on after death. Moreover, again, it is crucial that this soul is the "real person," far more important than the body in the determination of the self and its destiny. Indeed, certain medieval Christian sects went to the appalling lengths of flagellation in order to diminish the significance and even the worth of the body as it passed through "this vale of tears."

In the 17th century, René Descartes, often called the "father of modern philosophy," set out in perhaps its most famous

form the essentials of this dualist claim.[2] Without going into
the details of this subtle and important argument, we can say
that Descartes emphasized the same two crucial claims that had
characterized dualism from its first formulations: That the soul
or mind is a separate substance distinguishable from the body
(hence the "dualism") and that of the two, the one we know
best, the one that is most truly "the self," is the mind or soul.
Thus the "I" of the famous cogito, "I think, therefore I am,"
is an "I" which is a *res cogitans*, a "thinking substance."

As part of the metaphysical foundation of one of our major
religious traditions, as well as probably the dominant philosophical understanding of what a person is in the west, dualism
is obviously of enormous importance. Our vocabulary and even
our way of organizing our educational systems are steeped in
its assumptions. "A sound mind in a sound body," we have
been told for centuries, which clearly implies that we are this
combination of mind and body. Women, concerned that they
are being treated as sex objects, demand that they be respected
for their minds, and outstanding athletes must regularly fight
against the prejudice that they are just "dumb jocks." Following the recommendations of almost all the dualists mentioned
so far, we organize our educational system with the assumption
that we should train both the mind (the "academic" subjects),
and the body (physical education and "extra-curricular" activities), with the clear presumption that the former is much the
more important of the two. On the dualist view, then, and with
the fascinating exception of Plato's discussions of education in
his *Republic*,[3] sport, centrally (though as we have seen, not
exclusively) concerned with the body, inevitably becomes a
pastime of diminished importance. It is no doubt on such dualist
assumptions, for example, that one hears so much of "mere"
sport, that in many academic institutions less (or no) credit is
given for physical education, and that sports and physical education are some of the first activities cut in times of economic
difficulty in educational systems. The very fact that most of the
sports that go on in educational institutions are classified as

"extracurricular" (literally "outside the curriculum"), clearly testifies to the same set of assumptions. Since the mind and body are separable, and since the mind is much the most important of the two, the core of education should of course concern "the life of the mind," and the training of the body can pretty much be left to the free choice of each individual.

But there are fundamental problems with the dualist standpoint that have beset it almost since it was first formulated. Probably the most troublesome is how these two "separate" substances, mind or soul and body, the one material, the other presumably immaterial, can interact with such intimacy. My mind decides to type this sentence and my fingers obey its commands. Or I try to get my body to perform a difficult physical maneuver, say, a complex dive, and get psychologically frustrated at my failure. Perhaps I even suffer from a "psychosomatic illness." In both positive and negative senses, the mind and body interact in myriad ways which are notoriously difficult to explain on the assumption that it is a material body and an immaterial mind or soul doing the interacting. (Indeed, it is worth noting that the very phrase "the mind and body interact" already contains the assumption of dualism.) Descartes, to take perhaps the most famous example, resorts to the desperately question-begging explanation that the immaterial mind and the material body are joined at the pineal gland! This, as many have recognized, is hardly a satisfactory explanation. What are some alternatives?

MATERIALISM OR PHYSICALISM

Difficulties of this sort have lead thinkers as long ago as Democritus to understand the human being in a different way, as entirely body. This position is known as materialism, or more recently, physicalism. Its fundamental standpoint is easy enough to state, though the details are enormously complex. So-called "mental" activity is nothing immaterial or the mysterious manifestation of a soul. Thinking is no different in principle from moving one's fingers across a keyboard. Both are the result of neurons firing, synapses being crossed, nerves being stimulated. Everything about us, including our thoughts, loves, and anxieties, are founded in the physical. "Body am I entirely and nothing else; and soul is only a word for something about the body," says Nietzsche's Zarathustra in a succinct formulation of this position.[4]

Like the dualist position, the physicalist one has much to recommend it. Especially in an age dominated by the positivist assumption that one should only believe that for which there is "scientific evidence," the physicalist position avoids appeals to what can sometimes seem mystifying notions of souls or immaterial minds. Moreover, since science holds sway in the domain of the physical, if the entire human is indeed physical, then in principle everything about human being is accessible to scientific understanding. On the basis of this assumption, enormous progress has been made in understanding human mental and psychological events.

But it too has its problems, which opponents regard as insurmountable. Perhaps the most troublesome is that of "reductionism." To say that experiences such as "I think, therefore I am," or "I love Anne," or "I wish this day were over," are really nothing but a complex set of neuron firings and other physical events, seems to "reduce" what are qualitatively different experiences to the straightforwardly physical. I certainly don't experience, say, "I think, therefore I am," as a physical activity qualitatively similar to moving my finger. At very least, the physicalist position must explain the difference between material which thinks (the mind) and material which does not (the body). That, say its opponents, it is unable to do. The most the position can "prove" is that for every "mental act" there is a parallel physical event—say a given set of neuron firings. But a parallel is not an identity, or so say the critics of physicalism.

To use an example from the realm of sport, how can the physicalist explain the experienced difference between, on the one hand, the process of building up my aerobic capacity for the coming season by running wind sprints, and, on the other, "psyching myself up for the game" by an elaborate ritual of "letting the self go" and focusing entirely on the task at hand, or by thinking about how important the game is to the team? This has led certain thinkers to understand human embodiment in a different way.

PHENOMENOLOGY

By far the most well-received account of human activity among scholars of sport, however, is the largely 20th century movement known as phenomenology, of whom the German philosopher, Edmund Husserl, is often regarded as the founder. According to the phenomenologist, what needs to be explained is not some abstract notion of what a given phenomenon is "in itself," (without reference to the human experience thereof), but precisely the given phenomenon as it is experienced, or "as it appears."

The phenomenologist, when seeking an account, say, of friendship, or loneliness, wants not an explanation of the "unconscious" psychoanalytic roots of the experience, much less of the relevant neuron firings, but rather an accurate and adequate description of the experience itself, of its qualities, characteristics, and structures. Crucially, the phenomenologist claims that the way we actually experience ourselves is neither as a "dualism" of mind and body somehow mysteriously interacting, nor as a "mere body," but as a unity of mental and physical activity which phenomenologists often call "the lived body." The phenomenologist, Calvin O. Schrag, puts it thusly:

The phenomenon in question is my body as concretely lived. The body as immediately apprehended is not a corporeal substance which is in some way attached to, or united with, another substance, variously called in the tradition a "soul," "mind," or "self." The body thus conceptualized is a later abstraction and objectivization, which is phenomenologically eviscerated and epistemologically problematic. I experience my body first as a complex of life-movements which are indistinguishable from my experience of selfness. . . . The distinctions between soul and body, or mind and body, as they have been formulated in the tradition (particularly by Descartes) are reified and objectivized distinctions, foreign to man's experience as it is immediately lived.[5]

It is thus the emphasis on the experienced unity of mental and physical activity which characterizes the phenomenological position. More than that, such thinkers insist that human activity can only be adequately understood by thinking human experience as that unified whole, not by dividing it up.

An analysis of man's incarnation reveals that man is an opaque and partially concealed "body subject" without clear and precise points of demarcation for the various aspects of his being; he is a unity of physical, biological, and psychological relationships necessarily interrelated and only meaningfully investigated when analyzed as a whole.[6]

For the phenomenologist, then, the body is not to be thought of as an entity, which somehow mysteriously interacts with another qualitatively different entity. Nor is it an entity in the "objective" biological sense: a combination of muscles, bones, digestive, respiratory, reproductive systems, neuron firings, etc. It is not to be understood as an entity at all. Rather, we should understand and describe our bodies as we experience them, as they are lived, as what we are. So understood, our bodies, as the French philosopher, Gabriel Marcel, has insisted, are not something we have; I am my body.[7]

What happens when we turn to an analysis of human movement within the sporting domain? According to many, there could hardly be better evidence for the claims of phenomenologists regarding the lived body as a unity than in our experience of embodiment in sport. As we have seen in earlier discussions, precisely what characterizes most athletic activity is the fully unified co-presence of mental and physical activity, a unity so deep that the two components of the activity can no longer be separated. As I move toward the basket, see my teammate cut, and throw him a pass, or as I notice the spin on the baseball, recognize that it is a curve, and adjust my swing accordingly, am I "thinking" or "physically acting?" The only sensible answer seems to be both, together, as one.

Part of the enormous appeal of athletics is no doubt this quality, that our whole selves can be immersed in the activity, that nothing of us is "held in reserve." The experience which, as we saw earlier, is often misconstrued as acting "without having to think" is itself testimony to the genuine union of physical and mental activity in lived embodiment. The athlete, that is, does not experience herself either as a "two" a combination of mind and body somehow working together, nor as an elaborate set of muscles, bones and neuron firings, but, again, as a lived body, as a body which in its concrete life and activity is what I am as a thinking/acting being.

An interesting and thought-provoking qualification on this phenomenological account needs to be noted, however. The phenomenological account of the lived body unity seems especially appropriate for the successful experience of the skilled athlete, who, in the achieved unity of mental and physical activity, "no longer has to think," in the explicit analytic sense, about what he or she does. There the unity is manifest. But what about the novice, skiing for the first time, who desperately tries to remember all the instructions about keeping one's skis parallel, unweighting, etc., and transform them into action, usually with comical failure? Is the novice not one who has failed to achieve this phenomenological unity, for whom there is all too much of a "mind-body" distinction? Or consider the phenomenon of the injured athlete, perhaps a fine soccer player, usually adept at combining his mental and physical activity into outstanding play, but whose injured ankle now makes it impossible for him to cut or kick as he wishes. Is not such an athlete beset by a mind-body dichotomy which is alienating, and which he desperately wishes to overcome? It is worth recalling that Paul Weiss, in his *Sport: a Philosophic Inquiry*, characterizes this desire to overcome the mind-body dualism as part of the very appeal of sport for males, who, unlike women, do experience this alienating dualism.[8] If all this is true, however, it is not so much that the lived body as a unity is simply the way we always are, as phenomenologists usually insist. It is rather a special achievement out of the experience of dualism which, on this understanding, becomes a defective mode of human experience, but a mode nevertheless. That is, on this view, we would seem to be both dualist and a unified lived body, but at different times, and in a hierarchical order such that the lived body unity is a superior achievement, something for which we should strive as the explicit overcoming of the mind/body dualism which we often experience as alienating.[9]

THE PLATONIC VIEW

We would not want to leave a discussion of the connection of mind and body and its relation to sport without considering the special case of the Greek philosopher, Plato. Plato is often considered a dualist in the orthodox sense, although it is not clear that he actually holds to this position.[10] What is clear is that he wishes to use the vocabulary of soul and body when speaking of the human situation. In his *Republic*, in the process of establishing what Socrates calls the "city in speech" which is the perfectly just city, Socrates turns explicitly to the role of "gymnastic" in a proper education, giving that activity an important role indeed.[11] The two crucial elements in a fine education, he suggests are "musikē" (the rough equivalent of our "fine arts," and "gymnastikē" (the rough equivalent of our physical education). Any modern American must be stunned by the claim that these two pursuits should be the foundation of a sound education. They are precisely the two studies we place at the periphery of our educational system, the studies we give the least emphasis, consider least important, and curtail or even eliminate first during times of economic difficulty. For our purposes, what is especially important and striking is that Socrates devotes considerable time to the careful setting out of a sustained training in gymnastic as one of the cores of a sound education.

Then the man who makes the finest mixture of gymnastic with music and brings them to his soul in the most proper measure is the one of whom we would most correctly say that he is the most perfectly musical and well harmonized, far more so than of the man who tunes the strings to one another.[12]

Now if Plato were a straightforward dualist of the sort discussed above, one might assume that the purpose of this training in music and gymnastics would be appropriately divided, such that gymnastic trains the body and music the soul. But Socrates explicitly denies this. The connection is far more intimate.

"Then Glaucon," I said, "did those who established an education in music and gymnastic do so for other reasons than the one supposed by some, that the latter should care for the body and the former for the soul?" "For what else, then?" he said. "It's likely," I said, "that they established both chiefly for the soul."[13]

In explaining to Glaucon this puzzling claim, Socrates adds this clarification:

Now I, for one, would assert that some god gave two arts to human beings for these two things, as it seems—music and gymnastic for the spirited and the philosophic—not for the soul and body, except incidentally, but rather for these two. He did so in order that they might be harmonized with one another by being tuned to the proper degree of tension and relaxation.[14]

The point of gymnastics (as we might now say, of sport education), Socrates insists, is not to train the body—as an entity separate from the soul—but is part of the unified education of the whole person. A proper education in gymnastics makes one a better person, not just the body a better body. This can only be so, I suggest, if the soul and body are so intimately connected as to be virtually inseparable. The Platonic Socrates seems already to appreciate this intimacy of the mental and the physical that the phenomenologists today emphasize. On this view, the real point of physical education as education is not to develop only our bodies, but to properly develop our selves. Perhaps contemporary educators, in the same spirit, should rethink their own diminution of the significance of athletic education and the dualist assumptions on which it is founded, in favor of an understanding of the far deeper intimacy of soul and body, and a role to the "physical" in education that does justice to that intimacy.

In Chapter 3, on self-knowledge, we discovered that the categories of analysis by which psychologists such as Arnold Beisser analyze the significance of our sport choices were not of a sort that supplied definitive answers to the question of who we are. Rather, they enabled us to ask the kind of questions which, answered individually and honestly, might move us toward self-knowledge. A similar phenomenon occurs in this chapter. Sport, combining in such intimacy our mental and physical capabilities, offers a marvelous testing ground for some of the major theories that have been put forward to explain this intimate connection between the mental and the physical in human beings. Does it resolve the problem in favor or one or another theory? Hardly. But it does offer us that arena for asking those questions which can move us toward at least a plausible position on this important issue. And because, for most of us, the evidence of sporting activity is in some measure our own athletic experience, it can lead us as well to a position on the issue which rings true to our own lives, and so becomes itself part of the self-knowledge which it is the office of philosophy to seek. In the next chapter, we shall consider yet another dimension of the understanding of ourselves in sport, the connection of sport and aesthetic themes, such as beauty, grace, and elegance.

NOTES

1. Plato, *Phaedo*. I do not mean to suggest that this was in fact Plato's own view. Although that is still an orthodox interpretation, I would contend against it. We can say uncontroversially that Plato simply took up the view and examined some of its consequences in that dialogue.

2. See especially his Meditations on First Philosophy.

3. Plato, *Republic*. See especially Book III, page 410 ff.

4. Nietzsche, Friedrich, *Thus Spoke Zarathustra*, in *The Portable Nietzsche*, edited by Walter Kaufmann. New York, Penguin Books, 1982, page 146.

5. Schrag, Calvin O., "The Lived Body as a Phenomenological Datum," in *Philosophic Inquiry in Sport*, edited by Morgan & Meier. Champaign, Ill., Human Kinetics Publishers, 1988, page 110.

6. Meier, Klaus V., "Embodiment, Sport, and Meaning," in Morgan & Meier, *op. cit.*, page 97.

7. Marcel, Gabriel, *Metaphysical Journal*. Chicago, Henry Regnery Co., 1952, page 333.

8. Weiss, *op. cit.*, Chapter 13.

9. For perhaps the most extreme case of the mind/body split, consider a person in that form of schizophrenic episode sometimes called "delusions of grandeur;" perhaps a person sitting in an asylum room in a hospital robe, but who believes he is Napoleon.

10. This is an issue of scholarly controversy and would take an extended textual interpretation to resolve. To simply point a direction, let me say that the account of eros presented in the *Symposium* and *Phaedrus* cannot be made coherent on the assumption of a sub-

stantial dualism of soul and body. This does not deny, of course, that Plato would not want to maintain the vocabulary of soul and body; it only denies that soul and body are to be understood as two separate substances.

11. Plato, *Republic*, see especially Book III.

12. Plato, *Republic*, page 412a.

13. Ibid, page 410c.

14. Ibid, page 411e.

CHAPTER FIVE

SPORT, ART, AND THE AESTHETIC

One does not have to listen very long to conversations about sports before one will hear invoked the language of aesthetics. We hear of the "gracefulness" of a great runner's stride or a basketball player's long leap toward the basket, the "beauty" of a play nicely "choreagraphed" by several soccer teammates, or of a well-executed dive, the "creativity" of a quarterback who makes a great pass even though the original play has broken down. It is clear, in fact, that our discourse on sport is shot through with the vocabulary of the arts. And not just the vocabulary; in some sports, such as gymnastics, diving, figure skating, and synchronized swimming, explicitly aesthetic criteria are employed to determine the winner. A diver will win the competition if she is more graceful than the other divers, or a figure skater if her routine is more beautiful than the other competitors'. In sports such as these, aesthetic concerns are part of the constitutive structure of the sport itself.

Considerations such as these have led many philosophers interested in sport to turn their attention to this question of the place of aesthetics in sport. It is fair to say that two issues have been of paramount concern in the dialogues that have ensued. First, some writers have been so impressed by the presence of aesthetic concerns in sport that they have argued for a virtual identity relationship: Sport in fact is an art form. Other writers have attacked this identity as a misconstrual of the role of the aesthetic in sport. The first issue, then, is whether or not sport is or can be an art form.

Those who decide negatively on this question often are led to the second issue. If sport is not simply an art, yet if, as certainly seems the case, there is such a strong presence of the aesthetic in sport, what exactly and in detail is the relation between sport and the aesthetic? In this chapter we shall examine some of the major positions taken on these issues.

SPORT AS ART

Many athletes have characterized their sporting activity as an art form, and a number of philosophers of sport have supported that conviction in writing. Not surprisingly, those athletes most given to claiming that they are artists are often participants in sports where aesthetic criteria are not just present but determinative of the winner. Thus a number of figure skaters, including Peggy Fleming, Toller Cranston, and John Curry, have claimed that what they do is art, and have in some measure revolutionized the sport of figure skating by introducing more explicitly aesthetic movement into their routines. In addition some philosophers interested in the aesthetic dimension of sport have supported the claims of these athletes with arguments aimed at claiming that sport, or at least some of its instances, can straightforwardly be art forms.[1] Their arguments typically begin with a recognition of the strong aesthetic component in many sports as a basis for the identity. Especially in response to objections, however, their defense of an identity relationship gets considerably more complex.

The philosopher who has most consistently and insistently attacked the claim that sport can be art is David Best.[2] Because the debate has for the most part begun with Best's criticisms and the attempts of defenders of the view that sport is art to counter his objections, we shall begin with an outline of some of Best's major criticisms of the view.

Best begins by acknowledging that there is, or can be, a strong aesthetic component in sport. In fact, he adopts the distinction between "purposive" and "aesthetic" sports to distinguish between those sports in which an aesthetic element is a contingent property of the sport, and those where it is an essential component in determining the winner. In the purposive sports,

. . . the aesthetic is normally relatively unimportant . . . In each of these sports the purpose can be specified independently of the manner of achieving it as long as it conforms to the limits set by the rules or norms, for example, scoring a goal and climbing the Eiger.[3]

In the aesthetic sports, however,

. . . the aim cannot be specified in isolation from the aesthetic, for example, synchronized swimming, trampolining, gymnastics, figure skating, and diving. I shall call these "aesthetic" sports since they are similar to the arts in that their purpose cannot be considered apart form the manner of achieving it. There is an intrinsic end which cannot be identified apart from the means.[4]

Obviously, then, Best acknowledges that an aesthetic component is possible in any sport and even required in some. His point, however, is that the defenders of the claim that sport is an art form make too easy a move from the recognition of the aesthetic element in sport to the claim that it is an art. There can be an aesthetic element in all sorts of activities and events; we do not thereby categorize them as art. Sunsets and mountain peaks are certainly aesthetically pleasing, but they are not art. Similarly, we can acknowledge that there is a significant and in some cases even an essential aesthetic component in some sports without claiming that they are art forms.

Even the so-called aesthetic sports, Best argues, do not qualify as art, because there remains in them a gap between the aesthetic and the purposive, albeit a smaller one. There is still "an externally identifiable aim"[5] which distinguishes, say, gymnastics from a dance performance, namely, the aim of scoring more points in one's routine than the opposing gymnasts. Moreover, the contexts of the two activities, sport and art, are different, and, Best insists, aesthetic elements cannot be adequately considered apart form its context.

A graceful sweep of the left arm may be very effective in a dance, but the same movement may look ugly and absurd as part of a service action in tennis, or of a pitcher's action in baseball, since it detracts from the ideal of total concentration of effort to achieve the specific task.[6]

In addition to the dichotomy between means and end which can never be fully overcome in sport as it is in art, as well as the differing contexts of the two, Best argues that the two activities cannot be identified because of the crucial distinction between the artistic and the aesthetic. On the one hand, Best admits that what counts as "art" is by no means clear or uncontroversial. One can legitimately disagree, for example, on whether a "found object" can count as art, or more generally, on what the relevant criteria for an object's counting as art should be. Still, he insists, we also cannot allow simply that anything can be an object of art or any activity an art form, else the very notion of "art" becomes so vague as to be meaningless. One can agree that the particular boundaries which define something as art are vague or controversial without simply allowing anything to be art. In particular, he argues, for anything to be an art form, it must at least allow for the possibility of expressing attitudes towards life.

It is distinctive of any art form that its conventions allow for the possibility of the expression of a conception of life situations. Thus the arts are characteristically concerned with contemporary moral, social, political and emotional issues. Yet this is not true of the aesthetic. . . . It is difficult to imagine a gymnast who included in his sequence movements which expressed his view of war, or of love in a competitive society, or of any other such issue. Certainly if he did so, it would, unlike art, *detract* to that extent from his performance.[7]

Best asserts, by way of avoiding a misinterpretation of his position, that he is not denying, for example, that lots of dramatic things can happen in a sports context, even things which constitute a comment on contemporary issues, as when black American athletes extended their raised fists on the winners' rostrum at the Olympics as a protest against racial discrimination. Dramatic, even tragic things can happen to athletes, but they happen to the athletes themselves, not to the imagined persons whom the athletes represent.

It is an understood part of the convention that tragedy in a play happens to the *fictional characters* being portrayed, and not to the actors, i.e. the living people taking part. . . . To put the point roughly, it is a central convention of art, in contrast to sport, that the object of one's attention is an *imagined* object.[8]

Thus the dreadful events in a tragic play, say the blinding of Oedipus, happen to the character, not to the actor playing the character. But it makes no sense, Best suggests, to say of a football player that it was the fullback who was injured on that play, not the player playing fullback. This is simply one more characteristic which fundamentally differentiates art forms from sport.

Taken together, such considerations as these lead Best to conclude that the effort to claim that sport is or can be an art form is misguided. No matter how aesthetically pleasing some sports may be, no matter how important aesthetic criteria might be in certain sports, there will always be fundamental differences such as the above.

A number of philosophers have disagreed with Best and come to the defense of the claim that sport can be art. They take up his arguments one by one, and attempt to call them into question. Let us next set out some of the most important rejoinders.

Recall that one of Best's arguments hinged on his separation of means and ends in sport. Even if there is an aesthetic dimension in sport, he asserts, it is directed toward some purpose external to the activity itself, such as scoring points or goals. In art, on the contrary, the purpose or end of the artistic activity cannot be so separated from the activity itself, the "means." Thus, to use Best's own example, scoring goals is an external purpose to the aesthetics of how the goal is scored, and it makes sense for a coach to say that he doesn't care how a goal is scored (whether aesthetically or not) as long as it is scored. The analogue to the arts, he suggests, is the case of a person who buys a work of art as a financial investment; here, as in sport, the purpose is external to the activity itself. Joseph Kupfer, among others, has responded to this objection, pointing out that the "end" of scoring goals is in fact not external to the activity but built into the very nature of the sport itself.

> Scoring is not an end which could be accomplished by some other avenue because what it means "to score" depends upon the particular kind of game being played. . . . Scoring is not a purpose of sport but is an end within the play of the game, in fact, created as part of the game.[9]

Thus, he argues, there simply does not exist in sport the clear-cut means-end separation which would allow for the separation of aesthetic means and purpose that Best wishes to draw.

Terence Roberts agrees with Kupfer. He presents an extended argument against Best, based on what he regards as an equivocation in Best's analysis.[10] When Best speaks of art, Roberts notes, he concentrates on the *particularity* of each work, that each work constitutes its own unique expression. Best insists that any attempt to formulate that expression in more general terms—"this painting is about sadness, that play about man's inhumanity to man"—results only in trivialities.

However, when he turns to sport, as Roberts sees it, Best speaks only in general terms about "goal scoring," thereby ignoring the very particular significance of the specific goal that, in the case of the arts, he insisted upon exclusively. This enables him to assert, in effect, that one goal is no different from any other. How a goal is scored in sport does not matter, whereas in the arts, given his emphasis on the particularity of each work, such generalization is impossible. But, Roberts argues, Best ought to recognize the efficacy of the particular and the general in both art and sport. Best is right that each art work needs to be taken in its particularity, but he should also understand that there is a place for legitimate and non-trivial generalization in the arts as well. Similarly, in sport there is indeed a place for generalization (for example, when one simply gives the score on a sports program), but also a place for a recognition of the particular game, the particular goal, and how it is scored. By taking one side of each pair, Best equivocally draws a sharper difference between sport and art than he should.

Therefore, Best's claim that there are many ways to score a goal in the purposive sports but only one way to paint the painting can be seen as nothing more than an unfortunate manifestation of a fundamental equivocation. Viewed generally, there are just as many ways to express sadness as there are ways of scoring a goal; viewed particularly, there is only one way to express the sadness expressed or score the goal scored. Once the equivocation is righted, the differences vanish.[11]

The second aspect of Best's argument with which others have disagreed is his "contextualism," that is, his claim that whether a given activity is an art or a sport depends on its context and conventions. Since the contexts and conventions of art and sport respectively are very different, the two cannot be plausibly identified. Spencer Wertz has strongly contested this contextualist emphasis, arguing that although we should consider the context and conventions surrounding an activity, we should also consider the intentions of the actors. If we do, he believes, the differences between art and sport are once again more blurred than Best wants to allow.[12]

Wertz points out that, especially in our own epoch, the criteria for what counts as art are by no means well established or clear. All sorts of activities that in the past would be rejected as art are now included. There is even a movement in contemporary art known as "ludic art," the point of which is to develop games the playing of which is itself an art work. Thus, the relationship between the inventor of the game and the people who play it is analogous to that between a musical composer and the musicians who play the piece now and again. Given this looseness in the boundaries of art, and given, moreover, that all kinds of activities and objects, some of them shocking and even scandalous, are counted as art, it seems arbitrary to insistently exclude sport from this realm. "Having looked at 'sexual dancing' or art works done in human excrement, the possibility of sport as art seems downright tame—certainly uncontroversial."[13]

To a significant extent these days, whether a work or an activity is considered art is a function of the *intention* of the artist or person performing the activity. If, that is, it is *intended* as art, then it is art (though of course, it may be very bad art). For these reasons, Wertz argues, if athletes intend that what they are doing is art, there is no reason to deny that attribution.

If a sufficient number of gymnasts were to begin thinking about what they are doing as art and no longer just as "sport" in the non-art sense, this would transform gymnastics. This change took place with Peggy Fleming's aestheticism in the 1968 Grenoble Winter Olympics. People change all sorts of things they do and say about the sport. I think Reid is correct when he says that it is the players, the gymnasts, or the skaters, who will decide.[14]

So by considering the intentions of the participants as well as the context and conventions of the activity, Wertz says, the boundaries between sport and art will be further blurred, and the obstacles to considering sport as an art form weakened.

A third objection of Best to the claim that sport can be art was, recall, that art forms allow for the possibility of expressing "life situations," of making comments on the social, moral, or political issues of the times, whereas sport does not have that possibility. A number of writers have contested this claim.[15] They point out that expressions of attitudes, character, life situations, and even moral claims abound in sport situations. A gymnast's or ice skater's program might express exhilaration, sadness, or loneliness. In many if not most sport contests there are "lessons" exhibited from life itself, regarding courage, overcoming obstacles, "folding" under pressure, etc.

Like a novel, film, or theatrical play, competitive sports show us the complication of characters as well as their character, their inner fabric. And this yields aesthetic dividends. Consider the way fortunes are reversed, how the hero one minute may become the goat the next. Or the way some athletes rebound from adversity and some don't; the way one play can give rise to a stirring victory, a wonderful season, even a whole career.[16]

To this one might add some of the issues of social significance discussed in Chapter 3 regarding the sociological status of certain sports, the very playing of which "makes a statement." Imagine the socio-political impact, for example, if a group of black students at a predominantly white college were to set up a double-dutch tournament at the student center. Or consider the case of basketball, where a distinction is sometimes made between a loose, creative, individualistic style of play, labeled "black" basketball, and a more controlled, careful, less dramatic style, labeled "white." A player may "play white" or "play black" regardless of his or her race. Clearly, a statement is taken to be made here simply by the style in which one plays the game.

Best has attempted to counter these objections by pointing

to the fictional or imaginary element in some art. When Oedipus is blinded on the stage, or when Othello goes into a rage, we know that it is the character in the play, not the actor himself, who is suffering the action. But in sports such a distinction is not made. If the fullback suffers an injury, it is the individual player, not "the fullback" who suffers. True enough, but Best's example might be almost peculiar to the theatrical arts. We do not, for example, say that it was not that particular violinist but "the first violin chair" that expressed such sadness in that lovely adagio. Nor do we deny that it was this painter, say, Van Gogh, whose personal suffering contributed to such poignant expressions of passion in his paintings. In these cases, the situation with the arts seems more closely to resemble that of the athlete, who might also express something of her passion or personal standpoint in the way she plays.[17]

Best has, as one might expect, responded to at least some of these objections. Let us take a look at some of his replies, in the hopes that the debate regarding whether or not sport can be an art form will be adequately framed, though certainly not resolved.

Regarding his claim that in at least the "purposive" sports there is a clear distinction between the means to an end (usually scoring) and the end itself, whereas in art no such distinction is possible, Best more or less sticks to his original argument.

For instance, the end which at least largely defines the character of soccer, namely scoring goals, can be achieved by various means. It makes perfectly good sense for a soccer manager to tell his team that he doesn't care how they score, how ugly and clumsy are their methods, as long as they do score more goals than their opponents. By contrast, it would make no sense to say to an artist that it does not matter how she achieves the purpose of her work.[18]

In arguing thusly, he seems basically to reaffirm his previous position, without specifically addressing the objections raised by writers such as Kupfer and Roberts. In particular, he responds neither to Kupfer's insistence both that means and ends cannot be so easily separated in sport, and that in any case, the "end" of sport is itself not external to the activity but is itself a constitutive part of the game. Nor has he responded to Terence Roberts' observations about the equivocation between appeals to the general case in sport ("scoring goals") and the specific in art. Indeed, Best continues to speak of the effort to make generalizations in art as resulting in claims that are "merely commonplace or trite."[19] But since the reiteration of a position is not a refutation of objections, we have to say that on the question of whether a coherent means/end distinction can be made in purposive sport but not art, and therefore whether this constitutes a fundamental difference between art and sport, there is still open debate. The same is true about the relevance of the general and the particular in sport and art.

Regarding Spencer Wertz's objection that Best is an extreme "contextualist" who fails to take adequate account of the intentions of the participants in determining whether a given activity is art or not, Best straightforwardly denies that he is a contextualist of this sort. He affirms that there must be an interdependence between context and intention in any adequate characterization of the phenomenon in question.

In fact, I do not deny the relevance of intention. Quite on the contrary. My point is that the very possibility of intentions *depends upon* normal context of occurence; if such a context did not exist then the supposition of the relevant intention would be unintelligible.[20]

Nevertheless, Best continues to criticize Wertz for what Best regards as the latter's own excessive emphasis on intentionality.[21] What we seem to have in this dispute, although the polemical intentions of the two participants has obscured it, is a basic agreement that both the context or conventions of a given activity and the intentions of the participants are relevant. There is, however, a disagreement on the degree of emphasis accorded to each, with Best emphasizing context more than intentions, Wertz the converse. Put in this way, it is an enormously complex and subtle issue, in philosophy of art as well as in philosophy of sport, one hardly resolved by this dispute. But the disagreement can serve to highlight these two important questions: To what extent are the contexts and conventions of given activities determinative of whether they are art, sport, or both? And to what extent are these decisions a function of the intentions of the participants?

When Best takes up the objections to his crucial point that what especially distinguishes the arts from sport is that the arts allow for the possibility of expressing attitudes regarding life, he again essentially reiterates his claim that "the possibility of an imaginative portrayal, expression of a conception of life issues, applies only to the arts."[22] He cites once again the example of the difference between an actor and the character portrayed in a play, reiterating that the difference does not hold, say, between "the fullback" and the player who plays that position. However, as we saw, that difference may be peculiar to the theatrical arts more than a differentiating factor between art and sport generally. So once again, the question as to whether this does constitute a fundamental difference between art and sport is an open one.

Finally, Best emphasizes that many of his critics consistently fail to distinguish between aesthetic issues (which Best does not deny to sport), and explicitly artistic ones, a distinction which, claims Best, is and must be the basis of the difference between art and sport.[23] This is certainly an appropriate warning, since in any discussion of the relation between art and sport, it is easy and tempting to move from the recognition of aesthetic ingredients in sport to the claim that therefore sport must be art. On the other hand, this also means that Best himself cannot appeal to aesthetic issues as the basis for a distinction between art and sport. The challenge to anyone who, like Best, wishes to definitively distinguish art and sport would therefore seem to be to draw and sustain such a distinction without reference to aesthetic concerns, which, since they are clearly present in both art and sport, will only obscure the issue. Whether Best or anyone can succeed in such a project is still an open question.

One final point which might be raised in the debate regarding sport and art, one which, perhaps strangely, has not been stressed in the literature, has to do with the differing nature of competition in each.[24] One might say that whereas in the arts, competition, insofar as it is present, is usually regarded as a deplorable phenomenon which compromizes the integrity of the art, in sport it is one of the central appeals and virtually definitive of the activity. To be sure, there is competition among artists. The successor to a retiring principal cellist in a great orchestra may be determined by a competition among aspirants; the competition among a group of painters to have their work shown at a prestigious gallery may be fierce and bitter. But no one, I take it, would suggest that such competition is part of the essential nature of the art as art, much less that it was particularly desirable. Competition in sports, however, the setting of conditions which enable us to strive to see who is best, who wins and who loses, is an important feature of the very enterprise of athletics (though of course, there are sports, such as fishing or skiing, which can be done in a noncompetitive mode). As is often pointed out, the Greek word *athlon*, from which our word "athletics" is derived, means "prize." Few would argue that the competitive aspect of sports is peripheral, nor that sport would be so much nicer if it were not for all that dreadful competition. Perhaps, then, not the presence but the nature of the competition in sport and art is significantly different. In the case of sport, it is an often constitutive and usually positive phenomenon, in the case of art, an externally imposed and usually negative factor.[25]

In leaving this debate, we could raise another question. Does the issue really have to be resolved? For one thing, to differentiate adequately between sport and art, one would seem to need a clear and well-defended definition—or at least an adequate characterization—of "art" and "sport." Yet both are notoriously difficult terms to delineate. But one might argue, since all participants in the dispute seem to agree that there is a powerful aesthetic component in sport as well as art, is that not the important thing? Should we not pursue this important kinship between sport and art rather than worry about the differences? In particular for philosophers of sport, should our reflections not center on the nature and significance of the aesthetic element in sport, which everyone seems to agree is present?[26] In what follows, I shall set out a response to just that issue.

THE STANCE OF ART AND PLAY

We have already noted the most obvious manifestations of an aesthetic element in sport. In virtually all sports, we praise outstanding athletes for their gracefulness, beauty, creativity, elegance—we praise them, that is, in the language of aesthetics. Moreover, in those sports which some have labeled "aesthetic" sports, such as gymnastics, diving, figure skating, and synchronized swimming, the criteria for determining the winner are aesthetic ones. We now want to ask, is this where the affinity between sport and art ends? Or is there a deeper affinity which grounds the shared aesthetic vocabulary and, in some cases, the shared aesthetic criteria? I want to suggest that there is, that the artist and athlete share a fundamentally similar stance toward the world, a similar orientation toward things, a mode of comportment toward their experience. This shared stance might be at the source of the aesthetic kinship between art and sport that we have already noted. Let me now try to set out that shared stance.[27]

I suggest that the stance shared by sport and art is the stance of play. There is, in the paradigm instances of both, a fundamental element of playfulness which characterizes their orientation. What is that stance? Begin with what might loosely be called a phenomenology of sport experience. Taking your own favorite sport as your imaginative example, consider in that activity your stance, your mode of comportment, your mode of being, as you play. What distinguishes that stance from your more everyday stance toward things? I suggest the following: when I play a sport, the first demand laid upon me as a player is that I be far more aware of things, more open to possibilities, than is usually required in my everyday experience. Playing soccer, I am called upon constantly to be aware of the location both of my teammates and the opposing players. I must try to be aware simultaneously of the movement directions of my teammates—and what intentions those movements signal—as well as the position and movements of the opposing players in their efforts to stop us. It is critical to appreciate here that I must not merely be aware of where they all are, but of what possibilities those locations offer. Nor is it simply the other players to whom I must be more open. The ball itself, the goals, the score, especially the boundaries and the time left in the game (which define the game's spatiality and temporality), all are issues to which I must be open if I am to play well. As a contrast, consider the typical degree of openness to our surroundings, to those around us, as we walk from one class to the next, or from one store to another during a shopping trip. My claim is not that we are totally oblivious in the latter examples, but rather that in the sport situation we are called upon to exhibit a heightened openness. The first "intentional structure" in our phenomenology of play, then, is openness.

But I would hardly be playing soccer well if I simply observed what was happening with exquisite sensitivity. The whole point of my heightened openness, we might say, is to enable me to respond forcefully and well to the possibilities that arise. If I notice through the course of the game that I am a step faster than the man guarding me, the point is to respond to that recognition by cutting past him. Or if I notice that the man marking my teammate is playing him too closely so that my teammate suddenly cuts past him toward the goal, I must respond to that possibility by kicking the ball ahead to my teammate as he cuts toward the goal. Again, my openness to the location of the boundaries, or the time left in the game, or the score, is never idle. In each case, I will play well just insofar as I can respond appropriately to the possibilities that emerge. *Responsiveness,* then, is the second important structure in our phenomenology of play. Together with openness, it constitutes what I shall call the stance of play, "responsive openness."[28]

A few points of clarification or qualification must be made initially regarding my claim that responsive openness is the stance of play. First, I am not claiming that responsive openness is a quality that is totally absent from our non-playful experience. It might be said that anyone who is even conscious is at least somewhat open and somewhat responsive. The point is rather that in play the demand for those qualities is so heightened that they become central to, and to an extent definitive of, our mode of comportment. We are speaking here of a question of degree. Second, I wish to claim that responsive openness is not just one of the things that we do when we play, like obeying the rules or trying hard to win. As the very mode of comportment which we take in play, it is more fundamental, more foundational, in that whatever rules we follow, whatever specific strategies we employ, they take place within the context of this stance of play.

So much for a brief summary of responsive openness as the stance of play in sport. I now wish to suggest that a parallel claim can be made in behalf of the "stance" of art. That is, no matter what art form we choose, I suggest that as art it is characterized in part by a certain orientation that the artist takes toward things, toward the environment and the materials of art. That orientation or stance, I suggest once again, is responsive openness. Consider an example: As I walk through the woods surrounding my home, I pass countless numbers of fallen trees, logs in various shapes, limbs twisted in this way and that. I may notice them from time to time, particularly the more striking of them, but even those I eventually pass by. My acquaintance who is a wood sculptor, however, responds very differently. Acutely aware of the minute variations in the textures, the shapes, the species of wood and what the characteristics of each are, he sees the limbs of which I take such brief notice as teeming with possibility. In myriad ways, then, he is more aware of, more open to the qualities and the possibilities of the wood than I am. But he is no theoretical botanist, observing with sensitivity these qualities for no other purpose than to know. He responds to that openness by forming the wood into the work of art that it might become, a bowl or table, or perhaps an abstract work whose function is solely to be an object of contemplation, and of wonder. Toward the wood, then, what distinguishes him and makes him the artist that he is, is the stance of responsive openness.

What is a poet, if not one more open to the possibilities of words, of language, and more responsive to them? A painter's openness and responsiveness to light and to color astonishes us, as does the potter's to clay and form, the musician's to sound and rhythm, the dancer's to space, time, and the movement of the human body. The stance of the artist, out of which the specific art work will emerge, which makes the artist the artist that she is, is responsive openness.

It is worth noting that in art as in sport, one way in which this responsive openness sometimes gets exhibited is as the knowledge specific to that activity. We may call the painter's heightened openness to light and to color artistic sensitivity; the capacity to respond to that sensitivity in such a way as to paint successful paintings we call the artist's knowledge or technique. In like manner, that a Larry Bird or Magic Johnson is so much more aware of what is happening on the basketball court, so much better able than the novice to recognize possible plays and to respond successfully, is tantamount to their knowledge of the game. One might suggest that this kind of knowledge, this responsive openness present in sport and art, is one to which contemporary epistemologists might well pay greater attention.

Let me try to bring home the affinity of sport and art more

clearly with a specific example. For my sporting example I shall choose basketball. Basketball is surely a game which presents the player with an initial structure. The rules of the game, the boundaries, the location of the baskets, all literally inform the game, give it a structure which, by the way, is so arbitrary that outside of the game itself we would never assent to such constraints. Under what other conditions would you consent to moving with a ball only when bouncing it with one hand, and only within a 90- by 50-foot rectangle? To these constitutive structures a coach will typically add patterns of movement which the players should follow, designed to maximize the opportunities to score. But those patterns almost never are so rigid as to allow for one and only one possibility. On the contrary, within the pattern of movement each player must improvise. Is the man guarding me so attentive to me that he is unaware of the location of my teammates? Then I shall lead him so that he runs into one of my stationary teammates, and I shall be set free for a shot. Or is he so anxious to stay aware of their location that he does not keep his eyes on me? Then the second he looks away from me I shall cut past him for a basket. Indeed, much of the appeal of basketball has to do with the exhilaration and creative action available in improvising within given structures.

But improvisation is no less a central theme of many art forms. In jazz, in modern dance, improvisation is one of the definitive possibilities. A jazz group begins with a certain structure, perhaps a particular key or the statement by one of them of an opening theme, and within that structure the jazz piece becomes the specific improvisation that the group accomplishes. Indeed, we could virtually say that the success of a given jazz piece is identical with the success of the players' ability to improvise. I have seen modern dance performances where the structure set up is that each movement phrase must have seven counts; within that structure the dance is the improvization of the dancers. Or perhaps the only structure is that the dancers must maintain some sort of physical contact with each other—a dance possibility now called "contact-improvization."

My point is not to claim that all sport or all art is founded upon improvization. One of the basic differences between various sports and various art forms, I suspect, has to do with the amount of improvisation called for. Basketball is no doubt more improvisational than the hundred-meter dash, and a jazz piece offers more opportunity for improvisation than a rigorously scored symphony. Still, it is hard to think of a sport or an art form that is utterly devoid of improvisation. Perhaps one might suggest water-ballet, with its emphasis on the precise unison of movement. But has not the improvisation in that activity been commandeered, as it were, by the choreographer? And however precisely a musical piece is scored, the piece itself is the improvisation within accepted structures of the composer. Moreover, as we know, there is always room for at least some interpretation by the conductor and the musicians. So we can say that improvisation plays more or less of a part in every sport and every art. Its possibility is central to their appeal for many of us.

But improvisation is the call of responsive openness. It calls us to see at once how open we can be to possibilities and how responsive we can be to them. As such, and insofar as it finds in sport and art two essential realms wherein its possibility becomes thematic, it is testimony to the affinity between the two. I emphasize that it is the thematic character more than the mere presence of improvisation that is crucial here. One might observe, for example, that what was earlier admitted regarding responsive openness is equally true of improvisation; there is an element of it in many if not almost all activities. To be sure, but just as in certain activities, such as sport and art, the significance of and demand for responsive openness is heightened, so here, I suggest, improvisation is not merely present in sport and art but is an explicit theme of those activities. The very possibility of our acting well is often a function of our capacity to improvise openly and responsively.

THE KINSHIP OF SPORT AND ART

Nothing that I have said regarding the shared stance of responsive openness in art and sport is meant to suggest that the two realms are somehow identical. The debate about this, outlined in the first part of this chapter, will be continued by those who find the differences more interesting than the similarities. I have intended rather to emphasize the profound way in which art and sport share a similar orientation or stance toward the world, and how important and desirable that stance is. Nor have I meant to claim that this stance somehow differentiates sport and art from all or most other activities, such as being a surgeon, or lawyer, or for that matter a pickpocket or mafia hit man. All of these, within the context of their projects, also call for responsive openness. Once the kinship of art and sport is adequately established, a legitimate question will certainly be what differentiates them in their kinship from other activities that might share a similar stance. That is a complex question, and calls for a sustained answer.

To simply outline the beginnings of a response, one might suggest that four elements would be decisive to such a differentiation. First is the profoundly aesthetic dimension to both sport and art discussed earlier, derivative of the fundamentally sensuous character of both. Second and third would be the powerful thematizing, as opposed to the simple presence, of the finitude of temporality and spatiality in art and sport, and the challenge to turn that finitude into possibility. Many activities exhibit spatial and temporal finitude. Few are constituted in such a way as to make that finitude an explicit theme, a central issue, and so to challenge us to take that imposed finitude and turn it into possibility, the possibility of the game itself, or of the art work. Fourth would be a discussion of the theme of fun in both, again construed teleologically. Many activities are fun; relatively few are undertaken with fun as part of their aim, as art and play do at their best.

These are complex issues indeed. To prepare the groundwork for a more thoughtful consideration of them, we must consider in greater depth this stance of responsive openness as it pertains to sport, and what its deeper implications are. That will be the task of our final chapter, to which we can now turn.

NOTES

1. See, for example, Anthony, W.J., "Sport and physical education as a means of aesthetic education," *British Journal of Physical Education*, Vol. 60, No. 179, March, 1968; Reid, L.A., "Sport, the aesthetic, and art," *British Journal of Educational Studies*, Vol. 18, No. 3, 1970; Boxill, J.M., "Beauty, Sport, and Gender," *Journal of the Philosophy of Sport*, Vol. XI, 1984, (also reprinted in Morgan & Meier, *Philosophic Inquiry in Sport*); A particularly strong advocate of the claim has been Spencer Wertz. See, for example, "Context and Intention in Sport and Art," in Morgan & Meier, *op. cit.*

2. In a number of works. See, for example, "The Aesthetic in Sport," and "Sport is Not Art," in Morgan & Meier, *op. cit.*

3. Best, David, "The Aesthetic in Sport," in Morgan & Meier, *op. cit.*, page 481.

4. Ibid.

5. Ibid, page 482.

6. Ibid, page 484.

7. Ibid, page 488. The emphasis is Best's.

8. Ibid, page 489, 490. The emphasis is Best's.

9. Kupfer, Joseph, "Sport—The Body Electric," in Morgan & Meier, *op. cit.* page 461. It should be mentioned that Kupfer does not argue for the claim that sport is art, but wishes instead to emphasize the significance of the aesthetic in sport.

10. Roberts, Terence, "Sport, Art, and Particularity: The Best Equivocation," in Morgan & Meier, *op. cit.*, pages 495–507.

11. Ibid, page 503.

12. See for example, Wertz, Spencer, "Context and Intention in Sport and Art," in Morgan & Meier, *op. cit.*, pages 523–525, and "Representation and Expression in Sport and Art," *Journal of the Philosophy of Sport*, Vol. XII, 1985, pages 8–24.

13. Wertz, Spencer, "Representation and Expression in Sport and Art," *op. cit.*, page 10.

14. Ibid, page 14.

15. For example, Wertz, Ibid., page 16, Boxill, Jan, "Beauty, Sport, and Gender," and Kupfer, "A Commentary on Jan Boxill's 'Beauty, Sport, and Gender'," both in Morgan & Meier, *op. cit.* pages 509–518, 519–522.

16. Kupfer, *op. cit.*, page 521.

17. After I had formulated this point, I read, in the most recent issue of the *Journal of the Philosophy of Sport* (Vol. XV, 1988), the article by Christopher Cordner, "Differences Between Sport and Art," who makes a similar point on pages 40–41. This article is a nice addition to the literature.

18. Best, David, "Sport Is Not Art," in Morgan & Meier, *op. cit.*, page 531.

19. Ibid, page 536.

20. Ibid, page 529.

21. Ibid, page 534.

22. Ibid, page 533.

23. Ibid., page 534.

24. For one such discussion see my article, " 'When Power Becomes Gracious: The Affinity of Sport and Art," *Rethinking College Athletics*, edited by Judith Andre and David James. Philadelphia, Temple University Press, 1990.

25. See ibid for qualifications on this difference.

26. I cannot resist reporting the observation of a friend who is intrigued by astrology; the "fifth house" in the astrological chart rules over "art and sports!" Were the astrologists on to something?

27. What follows has been set out in greater detail in my article, " 'When Power Becomes Gracious:' The Affinity of Sport and Art," *op. cit.*

28. I shall develop this theme at greater length in the following chapter.

CHAPTER SIX

THE STANCE OF SPORT

We have already discussed, in Chapter 1, the enormous cultural importance of sport in America. Johan Huizinga, in his book, *Homo Ludens*, has documented at length that this is no peculiarly American phenomenon. In culture after culture, from primitive to modern ones, he shows that sport and play has been at the core of that culture. In our last chapter, we want to raise the question, why do human beings play? More specifically, what is there about human beings such that play and sport have such a significant and apparently transcultural appeal? I want to present one response to that question which I regard as plausible. It is certainly not the only one, and it may, of course, not even be the most correct one. But I hope it will at least advance the issue somewhat and serve to keep it before us. Whatever our response to this question, we need to keep alive the issue of what it is about human beings such that play has the great appeal that it does. This is perhaps the foundational question in any "philosophy of sport."

THE STANCE OF PLAY AS RESPONSIVE OPENNESS

In the last chapter, I began this project by setting out the rudiments of what I call the "stance of play," responsive openness. Let me review very briefly what I said there, then continue its development.[1] When we play, and therefore when we play any sport, we are called upon and call upon ourselves on the one hand to be as open and aware of what is happening in the game as we can be. It is important to note that this is an explicit demand conferred on us by the activity itself. Moreover, the need for responsive openness is not merely there, as it is for us in many activities. It is made thematic, by which I mean that the very nature of the game itself asks, how open can you be to whatever happens? How aware can you be of what is going on in the game and of what opportunities are presented?

On the other hand, openness by itself would be mere passive observation. The second initial element in the stance of play is responsiveness. Our play situations ask as well how responsive we can be to those situations and possibilities which our openness reveals. We must not just observe those possibilities with sensitivity; we must respond to them forcefully and well if we are to fully engage in play. Together, the two elements, openness and responsiveness, constitute the most elemental aspect of the stance of play: responsive openness.

Several immediate points of clarification need to be made. First, if I were claiming that the stance of responsive openness is unique to sport or play, that only in these activities was responsive openness exhibited and therefore that it constitutes a virtual definition of play, it would be a silly claim indeed. Lots of activities, certainly including art, exhibit responsive openness. Indeed, a minimal level of openness and a minimal level of responsiveness might be taken as constitutive of what it means to be conscious. Rather, play and sport are activities which in a particular and explicit way call upon us, not just to be "normally" responsively open, but to be so in a heightened way.

Second, it is worth noting that in calling the stance of play "responsive openness" we are characterizing it intentionally rather than extentionally. That is, one might try to characterize play or sport "extentionally" with a long list of the specific activities which constitute play: tennis, swimming, soccer, fishing, etc. This—I think it is clear—would be both impossible and not particularly useful even if possible. Instead, responsive openness attempts to capture something of the "attitude" or orientation of the actor when he or she is playing, what it is about the "stance" of play which makes it what it is.

This enables us to account for two exigencies that we should be able to include in our description of play. First, some activities which are not usually considered play or sport can become so once the people involved become, literally, "players," that is, once they take the stance of play. Consider the activity of washing the dishes, usually drudgery. But done by a group of friends at the end of a party, with one of them perhaps challenging the others to see who can dry the most dishes, it could easily become play or even sport (though one unlikely to make the Olympics). Second, some activities which are usually considered sport extentionally can, when the participants take an inappropriate stance, cease to be play or sport, even though the "motions" of the activity resemble those of a sport. If a football team goes out on the field with the express intention of starting a gang war between rival gangs, they may look like they are playing football, but they would not be playing football.

The third clarification needed immediately is that I am not attempting to "define" sport as responsive openness. A definition is successful insofar as it captures every instance of the phenomenon it defines, but no activities or entities that are not instances of what it defines. That is, a definition should be neither too narrow nor too broad. It can thus be refuted by offering either sort of counter-example: an example of a phenomenon clearly included in what is being defined, but excluded by the definition, or one included in the definition but not truly part of what is being defined.

Responsive openness as a definition of play or sport in this sense would be hopelessly broad. Many activities which no one would consider sport or play could be characterized by the stance of responsive openness: being a brain surgeon, guarding the President, building a bridge over a chasm, or less flattering, being a pickpocket or a mafia hit man. These all require responsive openness, but no one would consider them sport. In recent decades there has been fascinating debate about the possibility of defining adequately related terms such as *game, play, sport*, and *athletics*.[2] But, I emphasize again, I am not even claiming to define play or sport. I am attempting to depict its distinctive characteristics—what qualities are especially striking or strong in these activities. If some or even all these characteristics are shown to be true of some other activities, that does not in the least deny that they are striking characteristics of sport or play as well. Thus, to use an analogy, if my two sons and I are all brown-haired, blue-eyed, short, agile, fast, and very athletic, those constitute striking characteristics, a kinship between us, notwithstanding the fact that there are no doubt millions of other people with similar characteristics. They do not have to be unique characteristics to be nevertheless what characterizes us. So with sport and responsive openness.

Still, more can be said, both about the way responsive openness is manifested in play and sport, and about other qualities which, though again not unique to them, nevertheless are distinctive. First is what I have called the "thematic" character of responsive openness in sport. It is true enough that responsive openness is called for in many non-sport situations. But in those situations, doing delicate brain surgery, or building dangerous bridges, or eliminating enemies, the necessity of responsive openness is imposed, as it were, by the exigencies of our life projects. In sport, however, the call for responsive openness is in every case invented, by the constructors of the game, and invented precisely in order to demand, in new and perhaps exciting ways, the stance of responsive openness. Hitting a baseball, for example, is a specifically designed challenge to be open to the kind of pitch being thrown and to be able to respond with a properly adjusted swing. In this sense, sport makes responsive openness an explicit theme, an informing challenge of the game itself: "Let's see who can be the most responsively open."

I want to turn now to some other qualities which are highlighted with the need for responsive openness in sport. Again, none of these qualities, so far as I can see, are present only in sport or play. But they are thematized therein, made a central and explicit concern of the players by the very constitution of the game. I want to touch on the theme and thematizing in sport of finitude, of possibility, of freedom, of value, of risk-taking and trust, and of fun as striking and significant features of sport.

FINITUDE

Human life is deeply informed by finitude in myriad forms. We know that we are finite temporally, that we shall someday die. Our embodiment makes us spatially finite; we cannot be everywhere, or even two places, at once. Rules that we must follow limit our freedom, or so we sometimes think. Yes, we are finite in so many ways. But usually, that finitude is something we try to avoid, put in the back of our minds, or, when it forces itself to the forefront of our lives, try—usually unsuccessfully—to rebel against it. "Do not go gentle into that good night," advises the poet, Dylan Thomas, "Rage, rage, against the dying of the light." In general, then, our finitude gets experienced as what Sartre called a "not," something in itself negative and something not to be dwelled on but avoided, even fleed.

In this light, sport is a strange human invention indeed. For in sport we take our finitude in its various modes and make an explicit theme of it. We constitute our games so as to bring to the forefront those modes of finitude which we usually try to avoid and force us to encounter them head on.

Consider first the rule-governed character of most of our sports. We establish rules in our games which limit us in ways far more explicit and arbitrary than in our everyday lives, indeed, in ways that we would never accept except in the context of playing the game. In soccer, we cannot advance the ball by touching it with our hands; in basketball, we can only move with the ball by dribbling it with one hand; in golf, we can only advance the ball by hitting it with a club. We accept these limiting and arbitrary strictures willingly and even enthusiastically, if only it is part of the playing of a sport.

Of course, being rule governed is no more a peculiar or distinguishing characteristic of games than is the stance of responsive openness. One might say that almost every activity is governed by the presence of at least some sort of rules, laws, or conventions. But in our sports, the rule-governed element and the finitude it entails is made an explicit theme of the activity itself. Our attention is called to the rules of a game in an especially powerful way as we play, and we are called upon to respond to and in the light of that finitude. I know that one of the "rules of life" as a citizen is that I may not take other people's money without their consent, or physically assault someone with whom I disagree. Rarely, however, is the presence of such rules as integral a part of my activity as is, for example, the rule that if I am playing soccer I must not touch the ball with my hands, or that in basketball I must dribble the ball when I move with it rather than simply carry it. Such rules constitute the game, help give it its meaning, in a far more manifest way than the more general rules of everyday activity. In so doing, the significance of rules, both positive and negative, is called to our attention. Yes, rules limit us; but they also grant us possibility, the possibility of enjoying the sport constituted by those rules.

 A second manifestation of finitude, present throughout our lives but once again made thematic in our play, is our bodily limitation. As embodied, we are situated, placed, in such a way that we are always "here." We can never be elsewhere than the specific place that we are.[3] Moreover, the specific bodies that we have limit our possibilities even more. Our size, speed, endurance, and physical ability, all are explicitly tested in our play. In taking our bodies to their limits, we discover those limits with special force and are made to face up to them. If I am tall, powerful, but less agile than my smaller teammates, those qualities confer on me both certain possibilities and cer-

tain limitations within which I must play. When we play ourselves into exhaustion, or encounter in our play someone faster,
more agile, bigger, or more skilled than us, our embodiment
as limiting, as finitude, comes home to us dramatically.

Two dimensions of this bodily finitude deserve special
mention: the finitude of space and the finitude of time. The
finitude of space is made clearest perhaps in those games with
delineated boundaries. A soccer or football match can only be
played within the boundaries, and if a defenseman is closing
in on you as you approach one of those boundaries, that can
be limitation indeed. Baseball adds an interesting wrinkle to
this limitation of boundaries. A ball hit "out of bounds"—so
long as it is hit between the third and first base lines—is rewarded rather than "counted out": it is a "home run." But
spatial limitation need not involve boundaries in a rigorously
rule-governed game. The recreational skier, skiing down a
mountainside, is limited by the trees on the slopes, but also
guided and perhaps aesthetically moved by them. And the rock
climber has chosen a sport whose very meaning is to confront
and test the spatial limitations conferred on us by nature.

The awareness of temporal limitation is similarly powerful
in sport. Again, more highly structured games are perhaps the
clearest examples. In a basketball game of forty minutes (or
on a playground, fifteen baskets), the limitations of time are
felt with special force, especially as the game nears its end and
you are trying to catch up. It is striking how much more intense,
say, a tie score is with two minutes left in the game than a tie
score in the game's first two minutes. The intensity of the
waning minutes is the intensity of our recognition of the game's
finitude. We know that we have only a few minutes left, and
we play more intensely in the light of that acknowledged finitude. But the recognition of finitude and its significance is by
no means limited to games governed by the clock. It is as
present in a three-set tennis match, or an eighteen-hole golf
game, or for a fisherman whose day on the stream is brought
to a close by the impending darkness. Baseball, as one of my

students pointed out to me, again has a strange wrinkle; it is one of the few sports which, at least in principle, could go on indefinitely. In theory, one could play a tie game, under the lights, interminably, without reference to time.[4] But it is noteworthy that even here, we are usually forced to impose arbitrary time limitations in order to bring the game to an end. In all these cases, the limitations of time, present always in our lives but more opaquely, are made thematic, integral in our play, and we are invited to acknowledge those limitations as such.

POSSIBILITY

But part of what gets revealed about our finitude in sport is that it is not mere limitation. The reverse side of finitude, as it were, is possibility. The rules of games, which limit our moves, also make the game possible as the game that it is. To render finite is at once to de-fine, to grant meaning. My body, which limits me in so many ways, is also my possibility—or better, my possibilities. I may be small, but my quickness enables me often to go by the larger players; it gives me a role to play. The same is true with the limitations of spatiality. The boundaries of the soccer field offer the place of the game. Only within and in terms of those boundaries does the game take on meaning and become the game that it is. What would a game be like with no boundaries and no goals? I am told that in women's lacrosse, there are no strict boundaries. Why then, does not the team leading toward the end of the game simply give the ball to its fastest player, and let her take off across the campus? Presumably, because they recognize that, explicit boundaries or not, the game is only possible within the limitations of boundaries. With temporality, once again, the limits imposed by the time of a game also grant it meaning. Most of us have had the experience of playing a sand-lot game where, after a long time, the score is forgotten. Far from "freeing" the game from the limits of time, the game soon dissipates.[5]

We need the context of meaning which our temporal finitude grants.

That there is this strange intimacy between finitude and possibility, that, contrary to what one might naively expect, a certain mode of finitude is almost a necessary condition for meaningful possibility, is demonstrated in another way by the phenomenon of focus. I have suggested that within the context of a given game, the stance of responsive openness is a *desideratum*. We must be as open and as responsive as possible to the opportunities that emerge in the game. But if we are to play well, say, in a soccer game, we must not, during the game, be open and responsive to the political problems of the world, progress in a cure for AIDS, or even our own personal problems, all of which must be set aside while we focus on our play and the responsive openness for which it calls. But this is to say that responsive openness, in order to be efficacious, must be focused. It must be directed in a finite way, limited in its scope to the issue at hand. If one could imagine an infinite consciousness, one might also imagine a consciousness able to be responsively open to everything, to the whole. But that is not vouchsafed to finite humans. Our sporting experience teaches us that the genuine immersion and meaning available in our games is a consequence of that finite focus which enables us to be as responsively open as possible, but within a given context. The same lesson, less visibly, is present in our lives more generally. Try loving all mankind, or even ten people at once; noble aspiration indeed, but one bound to fail. Strange as it seems, humans need focus, which is to say, humans need finitude.

FREEDOM

What is this intimacy between finitude and possibility that we discover so clearly in our play? If we think of possibility in its connection with the notion of freedom, we find in the sporting situation a revelation about the nature of freedom that we all too often forget. It is easy to think of freedom as simply the absence of constraint; the paradigm of this sort of freedom is omnipotence. I would be totally free if I were subject to no limitations. An omnipotent god would be the ultimate free being, and we, in striving for freedom, strive to be like the god. And indeed, constraints, especially ones we consider arbitrary, often are experienced as denials of freedom. A limitation by one's parents as to how late one may stay out is a limitation on freedom. So is a race or religious qualification at a prestigious club, or being confined behind an iron curtain. Such examples clearly support the sense we often have that limitations are denials of freedom, not conditions for it.

But our sporting experience invites us to modify this simple view. We have already seen that the constraints that we impose on ourselves by playing a rule-governed game are arbitrary and sometimes extreme. Yet the experience we have of playing within those constraints is one of freedom. Strange paradox, that subjecting oneself to constraints more limiting than those of everyday life should be experienced as freedom, the freedom of exhilarating play. Yet that is what happens.

Sporting experience suggests that for us finite humans, the experience of freedom, in order to be meaningful, occurs within contexts. It must take place within a set of limiting conditions which a superficial analysis suggests would be impositions on our freedom, not enabling conditions of it. We need to consider whether the same is not true of life. Our embodiment, limitation to be sure, also is the finite locus of our possibility to be what we can be. Would we really be freer if we were rid of our bodies, as many dualists have claimed? Or would our experience in fact be less meaningful, less ripe with possibility, less free? And if we were freed from the limitations of temporal finitude, if we were granted immortality, would we, in joyful freedom from the fear of death, live our lives more fully and meaningfully, or would we, without the constraints of time and the stake it puts on the choices we make in life, sink ineluctibly into an interminable boredom, abstract participants in a game without an end?

RISK-TAKING AND TRUST

Perhaps one of the more controversial dimensions of sport participation concerns the phenomenon of risk. Most sports involve a host of risks, the most obvious being the risk of physical injury. Some of the more dangerous, such as car racing or rock climbing, are even life-threatening. Now the usual stance that we take and recommend that others take toward risk is that unnecessary risks should be avoided, indeed, that anyone who willfully indulges in unnecessary risks is being irrational. If someone walks alone late at night in a dangerous city when taking a cab was possible, or goes on a snorkeling excursion when they can hardly swim, or drives when drunk, we regard that as irrational. Its irrationality is precisely that unnecessary risks were taken. Yet, except in the most bizarre of circumstances, one never is forced to engage in sport. Sport, and the risks it clearly entails, is in nearly all cases a free choice of the participants. Is it therefore not paradigmatic of irrationality, just insofar as in it we engage knowingly in unnecessary risks?

Nor is the risk of injury the only risk implicit in most sport. We know that competitive sports, by their very nature as competitive, risk alienation. The line between intense competitive involvement and alienation is a delicate and precarious one, and therefore, inevitably, sometimes devolves into alienation. For many of us, especially given the rhetoric of some coaches and members of the sports establishment, the possibility of losing is a threat to our egos. We are taught by misguided coaches to fear losing, and therefore, when we enter into a contest that we might lose, we take that risk to our egos.

It would thus hardly be an exaggeration to say that sport is to one degree or another shot through with risk. Indeed, the

Old English word *plegan*, from which our "play" is derived, means "to take a risk." Is the sustained participation in sport, which informs so many of our lives, therefore an act of irrationality? If not, why is it that we take such risks, and under what conditions is it rational to do so? A profound question, one to which a definitive answer is hardly available. But let me tie the issue of risk to another theme, seemingly in contrast to it, but as I mean to suggest, in fact closely connected: the phenomenon of trust.

We usually think of trust in connection with the avoidance of risk. "You can trust your car to the man who wears the star," we are told, implying that to do otherwise would be irrational risk. To put your investment money in the hands of a broker or banker you can trust is, we suppose, a way of avoiding unnecessary risk. Yet our sporting experience suggests that the connection between risk and trust is by no means so antagonistic. In truth, one of the very conditions under which we do willingly take the risks of athletic competition, one of the conditions under which such risks might even become rational, is when the taking of those risks is founded upon a base of trust. Let me offer a few examples: Race-car drivers are notoriously suspicious of rookie drivers until they "prove themselves," and such proof has little to do with winning races. The rookie must satisfy the veterans that her driving can be trusted. If I am playing a contact sport such as football, I willingly risk injury. But consider how my experience of the game changes when I become aware that my opponent is trying to hurt me with "cheap shots." Or a third example: I am an experienced scuba diver, but when a friend offers me some dilapidated old equipment, I politely decline to participate until my own equipment arrives.

In all three examples we begin with a situation already shot through with risk, possibly the risk of life itself. It is not, therefore, simply the taking of risk, or even the amount of risk, that leads us to be reluctant in some situations. Rather, the examples show an altogether different parameter within which we are willing to take risks in our play, and outside of which we are reluctant or suspicious. That parameter is trust. Our willingness and enthusiasm for risk-taking play seems tied to an atmosphere wherein we are involved in a relationship of trust with the other participants. In the case of the car-racing example, it is trust in the rookie driver's basic ability as a driver; in the football example, trust that one's opponent is not trying to injure you (although of course he may); in the diving example, trust in one's equipment.

I wish to bring home how striking, even uncanny, is this co-presence of trust and risk taking that informs so much of our participation in sport. What is it about this trust, we need to ask, which makes us willing to take risks which, without its presence, we often avoid as irrational? The examples above offer us this suggestion: it seems that what we want is to enter risk-taking situations where the risk is as purely as possible one of chance, of the fates. It may well happen that in a car race with competent drivers there will be a serious accident; I will "chance" that, but not in a race with a bunch of incompetents who make an accident all the more likely. I may indeed get injured or injure my opponent in a football game; I'll chance that, but not if he is trying to hurt me. I know that scuba diving involves considerable risk; I'll take that chance, but only with equipment I trust to be dependable.

The subtle difference in the situations seems to be this, that we want to enter into precarious situations where there are risks which cannot be controlled or eliminated in advance. But they must be genuinely left to chance. We seem to set up situations where the preventable risks, or perhaps better, those risks whose source is something other than chance, are eliminated. It is here that trust is so essential. Then we enthusiastically take risks. To be sure, social conditions, such as playing on an organized team for a school or city, may bring pressures to bear which lead us to continue our participation in a game when this trust has broken down. But then, obviously, the game has become alienated, and thus, as I have argued, a defective mode of play. My point here is that the risk-full play that we engage in willingly and enthusiastically is usually informed by trust.

VALUE

Yet another issue thematized in sport experience concerns value. Lovers of sport may be tempted to say straightforwardly that sport is "inherently" good. But as we saw in Chapters 1 and 2, sport can as easily lead us to do dreadful things as wonderful ones. What about responsive openness itself, the stance of play? If we speak of athletes and surgeons and lovers exhibiting responsive openness, it is tempting to say again that responsive openness, and so the stance of play that it grounds, is simply good. But examples such as the pickpocket or the mafia hit man, no less needful of responsive openness to achieve their projects, sober us quickly. Responsive openness itself is neither inherently good nor inherently evil, but can become one or the other. Within the context of a given project, whether playing a baseball game, performing brain surgery, or knocking off an enemy, responsive openness may be something to be desired. But its initial positive value can be offset by our judgment as to the value of the project itself.

Responsive openness in the service of the perpetration of a crime is hardly praiseworthy. It is a good, we might say, but not the good. So it is with responsive openness in sport. Within the project of the given sport, responsive openness will certainly be desirable. But the sport itself, or the occasion for playing it, may be ethically problematic. Consider sports such as bullfighting, or the hunting of endangered species. These examples make it obvious that the responsive openness exhibited in our sports may be as ethically problematic as in the rest of our lives. Once again, as we have seen a number of times already, sport presents us not with solutions to ethical problems or with the key to "the good life," but with the ethical problems themselves.

FUN

Finally comes the issue of fun. "Fun" is a notoriously difficult concept to define satisfactorily, but most of us know that in its highest moments, sport gives us the experience of fun. We should hasten to add, not always. When games devolve into alienation, when we are injured, when we lose a big game perhaps because of poor play on our part, we may not experience such situations as fun. But fun is a *telos* of sport; when sport works, when it is the best it can be, it is fun. Fun too, then, is a distinctive characteristic of that responsive openness which informs our sporting play.

I have tried in these pages to set out some of the noteworthy and distinctive features of that mode of responsive openness which is play and sport, without, again, claiming thereby to uniquely define the stance of this activity. But we still must turn to another of the questions with which we began this chapter. What is it about human beings such that sport is so appealing? Why do human beings play? To ask these questions is to ask after human nature, obviously an immensely difficult and complex question. We can only adumbrate here one possible direction of response, in the hope less that all readers will accept it than that it will offer a plausible model for the kind of response that might be true to the reader's experience.

PLAY AND HUMAN BEING

It has been said by many a philosopher that human being or human nature is a paradox. If the term "paradox" is an exaggeration, it is only slightly so. For any attempt to think about the nature of human being confronts before long a series of contrary tendencies, tensions, which can very easily seem paradoxical. Let me now cite only a few of what I think are fundamental ways in which this tendency to paradox gets exhibited. Each of them, as we shall see, bears on the stance of play as responsive openness.

The first apparent paradox has to do with the tendency of humans to experience themselves as, on the one hand, incomplete, partial, and in need of fulfillment, yet on the other hand, as complete, whole, as an overflowing fullness. Both experiences need elaboration.

We experience ourselves, again and again, as incomplete, as beings who lack, and, as a consequence, who desire literal "fulfillment." This syndrome seems to contain three "moments." First, in what we might call the ontological moment, we are, we have our being, as incomplete in an indefinite number of ways. There is an ontological negativity about human beings; we are not autonomous. Our lives are inscribed with an apparently indefinitely expanding variety of needs, needs which testify to our lacks. But in this first moment is contained the second; we experience those lacks, we are conscious of our incompleteness, even if only vaguely. Indeed, the most self-conscious of us recognize our lacks as such, we understand something of what it is that we lack.

Third and decisively, as we experience those lacks we strive to overcome them. We have within us a drive, a source of energy, which leads us to strive for wholeness out of the experience of incompleteness. Thus, for example, I may experience an incompleteness of wealth, and try to overcome it by making a fortune in business, or an incompleteness of political power, which I seek to overcome by running for public office. I may experience a lack of self-expression, which I seek to overcome by creating works of art, or I may experience a lack of wisdom, which I can only overcome by becoming a philosopher. This syndrome of incompleteness, recognition thereof, and striving to overcome it constitutes in significant measure the kind of humans that we are. Am I a husband, father, teacher, philosopher and athlete? These testify to the ways in which I have experienced partiality and strived to overcome it.

But this incompleteness syndrome is only one side of the

story, and here the first of the apparent paradoxes comes to the fore. Often, even in the midst of striving to overcome experienced incompleteness, we also experience a kind of wholeness, even more, a kind of overfullness or overflowing, in which, as we say, we ex-press ourselves (literally, "press ourselves out"). We pour out something of ourselves, almost as a gift, to someone or to the world. Of all the human experiences, perhaps love and friendship are the most obvious instances of this co-presence of incompleteness and overflowing. Our love for another is founded in and attests to our lack, but it is at once a giving of ourselves, a gift of the abundance of what we are.

We can now suggest how play as responsive openness, and so the appeal of sport, is founded in this aspect of our natures. Suppose, to the contrary of what I have said, that we were characterized neither by incompleteness nor by that overflowing fullness which leads us to pour out ourselves. Suppose we were simply complete, that we "are what we are and not another thing." We would then not be called upon to be open, since, lacking nothing, we would need to be open to nothing. Nor, lacking the impetus of overflowing, would we need to be responsive, insofar as a response is just such an outpouring or ex-pressing of ourselves. Responsive openness, then, is founded in and itself an expression of our natures as incomplete and overfull. Play, it seems, is a natural consequence of what it means to be human.

The second of the apparently paradoxical conceptions of human nature may be more controversial, since many have argued exclusively in behalf of one or the other side of the paradox. But I shall argue, again, that we are both. I refer to the interpretation of human being as by nature monadic, nuclear, or atomic, and on the other hand, the understanding of human being as fundamentally relational. There have been many spokesmen for both separately, as well as monumental efforts to hold them together, however precariously, in a unified human nature.

According to the monadic view of human being, we are autonomous, independent beings, "monads," who to be sure may from time to time enter into relations with others, but whose essential natures are not informed by those relations. Note that this is not a view which argues that the culmination of human life is to become a hermit. But it does argue that our nature is constituted by factors to which our relations with others, positive or negative, are extrinsic. Typically, spokesmen for this view emphasize the place of autonomy, of independence, and, to use the language of certain existentialist thinkers, of "authenticity." In turn, this view can be stated descriptively (the way human beings *are* is monadic, whether we like this situation or not), or it can be stated teleologically (the way human beings are at their best is monadic, just insofar as they overcome an inferior state of essential involvement with or dependence on others).

The appeal of this conception of the individual is familiar to us all. The well-known "identity crisis" could be interpreted as the painfully experienced absence of this sense of individuality. None of us like being "too dependent" on others. Even in those experiences which would seem essentially relational, such as love, we are troubled when such relations become ones of dependency. The appeal of this conception of the individual, then, should be clear.

But no more so than its apparent opposite, which I have called the relational view. According to this view, our essential natures are constituted in a fundamental way by the type and quality of our relations with other people, and with the world. Many of the words we employ to name who we are—husband, father, teacher, philosopher—are names of relations with other people or things. The point of this view, in contrast to the monadic, is not just that from time to time or even most of the time we happen to engage in a variety of relations with others. It is the stronger claim that those relations constitute who we are. As with the monadic view, this view has sometimes been employed descriptively—this is the way we are, whether we like it or not—and sometimes, as for example with Karl Marx, teleologically—humans shall one day become genuinely relational once they overcome the limitations of their inferior monadic standpoints. The appeal of this position is no less strong than the monadic. The view that we fulfill ourselves with and through others, that we become who we can be through those involvements, is as old as the Dionysian ecstasy, as enduring as the phenomenon of nationalism, and as recent as a contemporary coach's exhortation to his players in behalf of teamwork.

Given the appeal of both standpoints, it is hardly surprising that many of the greatest thinkers in our tradition have argued that human being is both monadic and relational, however paradoxical that may seem. Let me try to add at least to the plausibility of that conviction by noting that there is a coherence between this duality of monadic and relational conceptions of the human condition and the dualities discussed earlier, the incompleteness/overfullness dimensions of human nature and the understanding of play as responsive openness.

To begin with the connection to incompleteness and overfullness, the monadic element of our nature has a clear correspondence with the element of completeness or overfullness. As monadic, we think of ourselves as embodying a kind of completeness. We are, or seek to be, independent, self-reliant. When we do enter into relations with others, the source is not our need but our overfullness; it is a gift of ourselves that we give. Conversely, the relational conception is commensurate with our self-understanding as incomplete beings. As relational, because we take on the being that is ours in and through our relations with others, we reveal ourselves as incomplete. We do not contain within ourselves the ingredients of completeness, we need others for fulfillment. Thus the conceptions of human being as incomplete/overfull and monadic/relational could be said to be co-primordial and reflective of each other. It is little wonder, then, that both appear as tensions, even paradoxes.

Little wonder, either, that play as responsive openness also can be seen as founded in our "bi-fold" nature as monadic and relational. Our openness to things, to others, is a consequence of our relationality. If we were utterly monadic, like Leibniz's monads, we would have no "windows" to the world, no need for openness to others. Our essential relationality calls for our orientation toward others in the mode of openness, so that we may fulfill our natures. Our responsiveness, in turn, flows from our overfullness, and so from what we are "in ourselves." The expression of our responsiveness may or may not result in a relation with others; but its source, again, is in what we are in ourselves, and so in our natures as monadic. Responsiveness is one word for this flowing out of our monadic natures to the world, this gift to others. Responsive openness thus flows from our double natures as monadic and relational at once. Again, it is our very nature to take the stance of play.

These two interpretations of human nature as incomplete and overfull, relational and monadic, in their connection with responsive openness, have hardly been adequately defended or grounded historically in these few pages. But I hope that they have been made suggestive and plausible as the kind of understanding which might make sense of the apparently trans-cultural appeal to human being of play. Nor would I suggest that they are exhaustive of the possible meaningful accounts. One might, for example, consider another duality, that of dominance or mastery and submission. We are often enough in life tempted to take the stance of dominance over others, or oppressed by the dominance of others over us. Conversely, a stance of submission, passivity, or "letting it be" often offers an attractive standpoint, especially when we experience the world as out of our control, when "things are out of joint."

If we turn to our sporting experience, we can suggest that the stance of responsive openness occupies a precarious balance between dominance and submission or passivity, a balance easily destroyed by leaning too strongly to one or the other extreme. The stance of dominance, for example, could be seen as an excess of responsiveness and a deficiency in openness.

Submission, conversely, an excessive openness without adequate responsiveness. Alternatively, we could say that dominance moderated by openness becomes responsiveness, submission moderated by responsiveness becomes openness, and together, in a precarious balance always in danger of polarization into its extremes, they constitute the achievement of the stance of play.

Again, such suggestions are intended only as such, as directions of thought in response to a need present in the philosophy of sport as in any enterprise that would be understood adequately: to ground that enterprise in a plausible conception of human nature, to account for the appeal of that project to human beings in their being. What counts is that the need be heeded, that we include in our reflections on sport, finally and foundationally, an account of human being which might shed light on the enormous and wonderful appeal to us of sport.

Whither, then, the philosophy of sport? If there has been one sustained lesson in this book, I hope it is that sport does not provide us with many answers to the issues of life, but rather provides us with one of the richest fields for asking the questions. In sport, we hold ourselves open to question in more ways than one. Focused, intense, passionate, sport calls us to take our stand, sometimes even publically, as what we are. If we will only reflect on that experience in depth, we may find in it the occasion for the richest and deepest asking of the oldest philosophic question: "Who am I?"

NOTES

1. The rest of this chapter will present in a simpler way what is set out in greater length and detail in my book, *The Question of Play*. Lanham, Md., University Press of America, 1984. See especially Chapters 4 and 6.

2. See, for example, Bernard Suits, *The Grasshopper: Games, Life, and Utopia*. Toronto, University of Toronto Press, 1978.

3. Martin Heidegger has made much of the literal meaning of the German word, *Dasein*, usually translated "existence," but with the literal meaning, "being-there."

4. My thanks to Richard Maloney for this example.

5. Which is probably why, notwithstanding their theoretical interminability, baseball games are finally "called" after a certain period of time.

SUGGESTED READINGS

Beisser, Arnold, *The Madness in Sport*. Bowie, Md., Charles Press Publishers, 1977. A psychoanalytic interpretation of troubled athletes and how their involvement with sport is related to their pathologies.

Brohm, Jean-Marie, *Sport: A Prison of Measured Time*. London, Ink Links Press, 1978. A radical critique of sport by a French Marxist.

Fraleigh, Warren, *Right Actions in Sport: Ethics For Contestants*. Champaign, Ill., Human Kinetics Publishers, 1984. A book that sets out the author's guide for "right actions" in sport.

Herrigel, Eugen, *Zen in the Art of Archery*. New York, Vintage Books, 1971. The original work that applies the principles of zen to sports.

Hoch, Paul, *Rip Off The Big Game: The Exploitation of Sports by the Power Elite*. New York, Doubleday, 1972. A radical critique of sport, concentrating on American sport.

Huizinga, Johan, *Homo Ludens: A Study of the Play Element in Culture*. Boston, Beacon Press, 1955. The classic study of the role of play in culture, from the primitive to the modern.

Hyland, Drew, *The Question of Play*. Lanham, Md., University Press of America, 1984. Sets out the author's view of the philosophical significance of play for human life.

Meier, Klaus V., editor, *Journal of the Philosophy of Sport*. The best journal on the topic, with many important articles on a variety of issues in the philosophy of sport.

Morgan, Wm. and Meier, Klaus V., editors, *Philosophic Inquiry in Sport*. Champaign, Ill., Human Kinetics Publishers, 1988. A comprehensive compendium of important articles, including many of those cited in this book. The best general collection of articles on the philosophy of sport.

Novak, Michael, *The Joy of Sports: End Zones, Bases, Baskets, Balls, and the Consecration of the American Spirit*. New York, Basic Books, 1976. An exhuberant appreciation of sport, with an emphasis on its religious dimension.

Postow, Betsy, editor, *Women, Philosophy and Sport: A Collection of New Essays*. Metuchen, N.J., The Scarecrow Press, 1983. A useful collection of essays on women in sport.

Simon, Robert, *Sports and Social Values*. Englewood Cliffs, N.J., Prentice-Hall, 1985. An excellent book which concentrates on social and ethical issues in sport.

Vanderwerken, David, and Wertz, Spencer, editors, *Sport Inside Out*. Fort Worth, Texas Christian University Press, 1985. A large selection of writings on sport, including literature.

Weiss, Paul, *Sport: A Philosophic Inquiry*. Carbondale, Ill., Southern Illinois University Press, 1969. The ground-breaking book on philosophy of sport, by one of America's major philosophers.

BIBLIOGRAPHY

Anthony, W. J., "Sport and Physical Education as a Means of Aesthetic Education," *British Journal of Physical Education*, Vol. 60, No. 179, March, 1968.

Aristotle, *Metaphysics*.

Beisser, Arnold, *The Madness In Sport*. Bowie, Md., Charles Press Publishers, 1977.

Best, David, "Sport Is Not Art," in Morgan and Meier, editors, *Philosophic Inquiry in Sport*. Champaign, Ill., Human Kinetics Publishers, 1988.

————"The Aesthetic in Sport," in Morgan and Meier, *op. cit.*

Bottomore, T. B., editor, *Karl Marx: Early Writings*. New York, McGraw-Hill, 1963.

Boxill, J. M. "Beauty, Sport, and Gender," in Morgan and Meier, *op. cit.*

Brohm, Jean-Marie, *Sport: A Prison of Measured Time*. London, Ink Links Press, 1978.

Brown, W. M., "Comments on Simon and Fraleigh," *Journal of the Philosophy of Sport*, Vol. XI, 1984.

————"Ethics, Drugs, and Sport," *Journal of the Philosophy of Sport*, Vol. VII, 1980, page 15.

————"Paternalism, Drugs, and the Nature of Sports," *Journal of the Philosophy of Sport*, Vol. XI, 1984.

Buber, Martin, *I And Thou*. New York, Charles Scribner's Sons, 1958.

Camus, Albert, *Resistance, Rebellion, and Death*. New York, Alfred Knopf, 1961.

Cordner, Christopher, "Differences Between Sport and Art," *Journal of the Philosophy of Sport*, Vol. XV, 1988.

Descartes, René, *Meditations on First Philosophy*, in *Descartes: Selected Philosophical Writings*, translated by Cottingham, Stoothoff, and Murdoch. Cambridge, Mass., Cambridge University Press, 1988.

Diogenes Laertius, *The Lives and Opinions of Eminent Philosophers*. London, Henry G. Bohn, 1853.

Gilbert and Williamson, "Sports are Unfair to Women," *Sports Illustrated*, May 28, 1973.

Herrigel, Eugen, *Zen in the Art of Archery*. New York, Vintage Books, 1971.

Hoch, Paul, *Rip Off the Big Game: The Exploitation of Sports by the Power Elite*. New York, Doubleday, 1972.

Huizinga, Johan, *Homo Ludens: A Study of the Play Element in Culture*. Boston, Beacon Press, 1950.

Hyland, Drew A., "Competition and Friendship," in Morgan and Meier, *op. cit.*, page 231.

———"Competition, Friendship, and Human Nature," in *Women, Philosophy, and Sport*, edited by Betsy Postow. Metuchen, N.J., Scarecrow Press, 1983, page 162.

———*The Question of Play*. Lanham, Md., University Press of America, 1984.

———" 'When Power Becomes Gracious': The Affinity of Sport and Art," in *Rethinking College Athletics*, edited by Judith Andrew and David James. Philadelphia, Temple University Press, 1990.

Kupfer, Joseph, "A Commentary on Jan Boxill's 'Beauty, Sport, and Gender,' " Morgan and Meier, *op. cit.*, page 519.

———"Sport—The Body Electric," in Morgan and Meier, *op. cit.*, page 455.

Lasch, Christopher, "The Degradation of Sport," in Morgan and Meier, *op. cit.*, page 403.

Lingus, Alphonso, "Orchids and Muscles," in Morgan and Meier, *op. cit.*, page 125.

Marcel, Gabriel, *Metaphysical Journal*. Chicago, Henry Regnery, 1952.

Marx, Karl, *The Portable Marx*. New York, Penguin Books, 1983.

Meier, Klaus V. "Embodiment, Sport, and Meaning," in Morgan and Meier, *op. cit.*, page 97.

Mill, J. S. *On Liberty*. Indianapolis, Hackett Publishing, 1978.

Morgan, Wm., "Play, Utopia, and Dystopia: Prologue to a Ludic Theory of the State," Morgan and Meier, *op. cit.*, page 419.

Morgan, Wm. and Meier, Klaus V., *Philosophic Inquiry in Sport*. Champaign, Ill., Human Kinetics Publishers, 1988.

Nietzsche, Friedrich, *Philosophy in the Tragic Age of the Greeks*. Chicago, Gateway Editions, 1962.

——*Thus Spoke Zarathustra*, in *The Portable Nietzsche*. New York, Penguin Books, 1982.

Plato, *Laws*, in *The Collected Dialogues of Plato*, edited by Hamilton and Cairns. New York, Pantheon Books, 1961.

——*Phaedo*, Hamilton and Cairns, *op. cit.*

——*Phaedrus*, Hamilton and Cairns, *op. cit.*

——*Republic*, Hamilton and Cairns, *op. cit.*

——*Symposium*, Hamilton and Cairns, *op. cit.*

Postow, Betsy, "Women and Masculine Sports," *Journal of the Philosophy of Sport*, Vol. VII, 1980, page 51.

Ravizza, Kenneth, "A Subjective Study of the Athlete's Greatest Moment in Sport," paper presented at Mouvement, Actes du 7e symposium en apprentissage psycho-moteur et psychologie du sport, Octobre, 1975.

Reid, L. A. "Sport, the Aesthetic, and Art," *British Journal of Educational Studies*, Vol. 18, No. 3, 1970.

Roberts, Terence, "Sport, Art, and Particularity: The Best Equivocation," Morgan and Meier, *op. cit.*, page 495.

Sartre, Jean-Paul, *Being and Nothingness: An Essay in Phenomenological Ontology*. New York, Philosophical Library, 1956.

Schrag, Calvin O., "The Lived Body as a Phenomenological Datum," Morgan and Meier, *op. cit.*, page 110.

Scott, Jack, *The Athletic Revolution*. New York, Free Press, 1971.

Shainberg, Laurence, "Finding the 'Zone,' " *New York Times Magazine*, April 9, 1989.

Simon, Robert, *Sports and Social Values*. Englewood Cliffs, N.J., Prentice-Hall, 1985.

Suits, Bernard, *The Grasshopper: Games, Life, and Utopia*. Toronto, University of Toronto Press, 1978.

Weiss, Paul, *Sport: A Philosophic Inquiry*. Carbondale, Ill., Southern Illinois University Press, 1969.

Wertz, Spencer, "Context and Intention in Sport and Art," Morgan and Meier, *op. cit.*, page 523.

———"Representation and Expression in Sport and Art," *Journal of the Philosophy of Sport*, Vol. XII, 1985, page 8.

Wittgenstein, Ludwig, *Philosophical Investigations*. New York, MacMillan Co., 1953.

Young, Iris Marion, "The Exclusion of Women From Sport: Conceptual and Existential Dimensions," Morgan and Meier, *op. cit.*, page 335.

INDEX